Grandma Bellino's Italian Cookbook

Daniel Bellino Z

by The Same Author

La TAVOLA

SUNDAY SAUCE

THE FEAST of The 7 FISH

SEGRETO ITALIANO

GOT ANY KAHLUA ?
aka
The Big Lebowski Cookbook

Grandma Bellino's Italian Cookbook

Recipes From My Sicilian Grandmother

Daniel Bellino Z

Daniel Bellino Z

Broadway Fifth Press
New York, NY
Grandma Bellino's Italian Cookbook
Copyright © 2015 by Daniel Bellino-Zwicke.

All rights reserved. Printed in the United States of America.

No part of this book may be used or reproduced in any manner whatsoever without written permission except in the case of brief quotations embodied in critical articles and review.

First Edition
First Edition Broadway Fifth Press 2015
New York, New York
Cover Design Daniel Bellino-Zwicke
Cover photo property of Daniel Bellino Zwicke
First Published by Broadway Fifth Press 2015
New York, New York 10014

Library of Congress Cataloging-in-Publication Data, Zwicke Bellino, Daniel
Gandma Bellino's Cookbook
Recipes From My Sicilian Grandmother

ISBN- 10: 1508692319
ISBN- 13: 978-1508692317

1. Zwicke Bellino, Daniel, Cooks – New York (State)—New York—Nonfiction, I Title

All Rights Reserved …

Grandma Bellino's Italian Cookbook

Daniel Bellino Z

A Tavola si sta Sempre
in Allegria !

At the Table
one is always Happy

Grandma Bellino's Italian Cookbook

For My Mother

LUCIA BELLINO

&

NONNA GIUSEPPINA

Daniel Bellino Z

CONTENTS

INTRO ... To The Reader page 12 ... *Nonna* page 16 ... Sundays at The Bellino House page 21 ...

ANTIPASTO *page 26* ... Caponatina *page 28* ... Sicilian Stuffed Peppers *page 30* ... *Arancini* – Sicilian Rice Balls *page 32* ... Sicilian Stuffed Artichokes *page 36* ... Eggplant Beccaficio *page 40* ... Eggplant Sotto' Olio *page 44* ... *Polpo* – Octopus Salad *page 46* ... Clams Posillipo *page 48* ... Stuffed Mushrooms al Generosa *page 50* ... Sausage Stuffed Mushrooms *page 52* ... Spinach Artichoke Tart page 54 ... *Pollpette* - Sweet & Sour Sicilian Meatballs *pg 56* Pomodoro Repieno – Chicken Stuffed Tomatoes *pg 59* ... Insalata di Nonna *pg 62* .. Potato Green Bean Salad *pg 65* ...*Insalata di Ceci* – Chickpea Salad *page 66* ... Secret Salad Dressing *page 67* ... Insalata Siciliana *page 68* ... Insalata di Tonno – Tuna & Bean Salad *page 70* ... Sicilian Cauliflower Salad *page 74* ....

ZUPPE *pg 77* .. Zuppa di Lenticchie – Lentil Soup *pg 80* . Zuppa di Cucuzza "Gagootz" *page 84* .. Zuppa di Ceci – Chickpea Soup *page 87* ... Nonna's Chicken Soup *pg 90* .. *Zuppa di Scarola* - Cousin Tony's Escarole & Bean Soup page 92 .. *Maccu* – Sicilian Fava Bean Soup *pg 94* .. Sicilian Beef & Lima Bean Soup *p 96* Zuppa di Giuseppina's *98* .

PASTA *page 101* .. *Salsa di Pomodoro* – Grandma's Tomato Sauce *pg 104* ... Spaghetti Pomodoro – Spaghetti Tomato Sauce pg 106 ... Spaghetti Meatballs *pg 110* ... Spaghetti Aglio Olio e Accchiughe – Spaghetti with Garlic Oil & Anchovies a.k.a. Al Pacino's & Aglio Olio page 113 ... Pasta al Norma *page 116* ... Pasta Cucuzza a.k.a *Gagootz* p. 120 .. Pasta Lenticchie page 123 …. Cavatappi with Eggplant & Sausage page 126 .. Spaghetti & Broccoli *p 128*

Spaghetti Picchi Pacchiu – Spaghetti w/ Cherry Tomatoes *p 130*   Pasta & Potatoes *page 132* …… Ziti w/ Cabbage & Sausage *page 134* … Maccheroni w/ Cauliflower *page 135* … Pasta Pesto Trapanese *page 137* ….. Pasta Giuseppina *page 138* …… Spaghetti w/ Zucchini *page 140* … Spaghetti con Tonno *page 142* … *Linguine con Cozze* – Linguine w/ Mussels *page 144* … Pasta con Sarde *page 146* … Saint Joseph's Day Pasta *pg 150* .. Linguine with Shrimp alla Umberto's *p 152* … Mezze Monica al Contadina *page 155* … *Gravy page 158* .. Timballo di Aneletti – Sicilian Baked Maccheroni *p. 162* .. Lasagna Cacati   *page 166* … Grandma's Chicken Gravy Pasta   *page 169* … Lasagna Carnevale *pg 172* .. Maccheroni con Salsiccia *pg 175* … Ziti con Sugo di Agnello *page 177* .. Ragu alla Siciliana *page 180*

SECONDI … Eggplant Parmigiano *page 184* … Lucia's Stuffed Peppers *page 186*   Riso con Cucuzza Carni *page 188* …

PESCE *page 192* … Messina Style Swordfish page *194* … Pesce al Lucia *page 196* … Pesce alla Siciliana *page 198* … Mussels Marinara *page 200* … Shrimp with Garlic & Oil *page 202* …

MEAT & CHICKEN *page 204* … *Puttine* - Pork Ribs & Sausage *page 206* .. Braciola   page *210* …. Sunday Gravy *page 214* …… Chicken Cacciatore *page 215* …. Grandpa's Shoemaker Chicken *page 217* … Lemon Chicken *page 220* …*Chicken Marsala page 222* … Chicken Cutlets   *page 224* ….. Nonna's Roast Rabbit page 226 ….. Braised Rabbit Siracusana *page 229* … Sausage and Beans *page 231* …... Cauliflower & Sausage *pg. 234* .. Braised Lamb Shanks *page 236* .. Steak Palermo *pg 238* .. Grandma's Sicilian Meatloaf *pg 242* .. Stuffed Cabbage p *245* .. Italian Beef Stew *pg 247* .. Uncle Tony's Veal Marsala *pg. 250* .. Pork Chops *p 253* .. … Grandma's Veal Stew *page 255* …

VEGETABLES *pg. 258* .. Fritteddi *pg. 260* .. Scarola *p 262* Broccoli Rabe *pg. 263* … Zucchini Pomodorini *pg 265* Roast Potatoes *page 266* … Cannazzo – Sicilian Roast Vegetables *page 267* …

ITALIAN SANDWICHES *pg 268* . PEP & EGGS *pg 271* The Aunt Helen Special *pg 274* .. Sausage & Peppers *pg 276* Frittata Palermintana *pg 278* … Frittata alla Nonna *page 280*

DOLCI … Aunt Fran's Ricotta Cookies *pg 282* .. Bazzy's Italian Wedding Cookies page 284 … Neapolitan Lemon Cookies *page 286* … Zabione *page 288* …

ESPRESSO NAPOLETANA .. How to Make Espresso with a Napoletana Espresso Pot *page 290* …

Grandma Bellino's Italian Cookbook

BENVENUTO !!!

Daniel Bellino Z

Grandma Bellino's Italian Cookbook

Mancia di Sanu e Vivi di Malatu

*Eat with Gusto,
but Drink in Moderation*

Sicilian Proverb

To The Reader

First of all, I *thank you* for obtaining this book. It is truly an honor for me that people read and hopefully like my books, and I'm honored by each and every person who does so, so again I *Thank You*. I cook with love, as my mother, and my grandmother before her, and my Aunts Fran & Helen have always done. It was from my mother and my aunts Helen & Fran that I acquired my love of great Italian Food, first eating it, then learning to cook it, and the joy and love it gave me to make and serve it to others, and now to write about it. When I say, *Cooking with Love*, I mean it. That's what I've always felt when my mother put a gorgeous Stuffed Artichoke down before me, and the joy I felt upon seeing it, digging in and eating it. There is nothing in this world quite like eating a Sicilian Stuffed Artichoke, and as a young boy, it was for me the most supreme culinary adventure of all. You pick the leaves off, put them between your front teeth, bite down onto the Artichoke Leaf, you pull it forward, thus scraping the meat of the leaf and any breadcrumb stuffing that cling to it off the leaf and into your mouth. You do this over-and-over until all the leaves are gone, and you're down to the final treasure, the Heart of The Artichoke. Yum! This is the joy of eating a Stuffed Artichoke! And I've done it hundreds of times, but no artichokes ever tasted as good as the ones my mother made, and they were always a greatly anticipated special treat. My mother learned to make these Stuffed Artichokes from her mother, my grandmother Giuseppina. I learned to make them from my mother, Lucia.

Mostly all the recipes in this book are from my mother's mother, my grandmother Giuseppina Salemi Bellino. There are a few recipes that are not from her, but at least 92% are hers and the other few are from other members of the Bellino Family, my Nonna's offspring and grandchildren like me, my sister Barbara, cousin (cujino) Anthony and others. And most (85%) of the recipes are Sicilian, but not all. Once my grandparents Philipo & Giuseppina immigrated to the United States and settled into the Italian enclave of Lodi, New Jersey, nonna had some other Italian immigrant friends from other parts of Italy. There were mostly Sicilian and Neapolitan immigrants in Lodi, but there were people from Calabria, Genoa (Genoese), and Apulia as well. Nonna had her recipes that she made from her town Lercara Friddi Sicily, and brought to Lodi to cook for her husband Philipo and her children; Frank, Tony, James, Lilly, along with my mother Lucia. Yes, my nonna Giuseppina came to America armed with her seeds to grow Cucuzza, one special knife, clothes, a few photos, trinkets, and her Sicilian Recipes. She made friends, and along the way, Giuseppina and her Neapolitan and other Italian friends traded recipes. The Neapolitans from Napoli and its environs had especially wonderful food with great recipes that Giuseppina got from her new found amici. So along with mostly Sicilian

Recipes, there are recipes from Calabria, Genoa, Rome, and Naples as well.

There are recipes in every food category, like; Antipasti, Soups, Pasta, Fish, Poultry, Meat, and Desserts, but you'll find that there are more soup (Zuppe) and Pasta (Maccheroni) recipes than those of any other category. These were the foods that made up the bulk of the Bellino Family meals way back then at the turn of the Century and into the; 20's, 30's, 40's, and 1950's and the first half of the 20th Century in Italian America.

Soups were easy and economical to make, as were pasta sauces and maccheroni dishes, so they were made most often. Stewes dishes like; Stufato di Manzo (Beef Stew) and Chicken Cacciatore were a distant third in popularity to the soup and pasta dishes, but they were loved just as much, even more, as they were special more expensive treats, and not everyday fare, but for Sundays & Holidays.

 Desserts weren't eaten as much in the home of my grandparents, but once in a while they became a special treat for my mother, her brothers and sister Lilly. Once my aunts and uncles became adults however, and had children, desserts and the dessert course was a much bigger event than in my grandparent's day. When we went over to one of my aunts and uncles homes for a big Bellino Family Dinner, and once the main course plates were cleared from the table, it was then on-to dessert and coffee, the biggest and longest course of all. There was always a huge array of sweets on the table, both homemade by my aunts and some from the local bakery. The assortment of sweets was always a large one. There was usually a couple cakes from my aunts and pastries from the bakery, that only the bakery could make. Thing like Sfogiatelle, Cannoli, and Rhum Baba along with an assortment of Italian Cookies from the bakery, and possibly my Aunt Fran's justly famous Ricotta Cookies, which I loved more than anything.

One, thing I almost forgot to mention, while on the subject of desserts (Dolci). In Italy, yes they do love desserts, but most often, Italians in Italy, just like wirth my Nonna Giuseppina, they tended to have just some nice fresh fruit, like; Cherries, Peaches, Grapes, or Oranges after dinner, rather than sweets. Desserts were more of a special treat just once or twice a week, if they were lucky. And as concerns the Italians in Italy, especially in cities like Rome, Florence, and Naples, sometimes when a family has dinner at home, they might choose to, again for a special treat, go out for dessert at the local Gelateria or Pasticceria, or Caffe. Basta!

So now my dear readers, these are the recipes from my Sicilian Grandmother Giuseppina.

I do hope you enjoy!
Daniel

NONNA

My Nonna Giuseppina came to America through Ellis Island, New York in 1904 with my maternal grandfather Philipo Bellino. They both came from Lercara Friddi, Sicily, a small town about 40 minutes south of Palermo. They came here for a better life in America, just like millions of other Italian immigrants at the time (1890 – 1920). They left Italy because it was a very poor country, and they themselves were poor and had heard of this better life for everyone in America where the streets were paved with Gold, or so they thought. My grandparents settled in Yorkville on the Upper East Side of Manhattan and lived there for a few years. After the first few years in New York my Grandfather Philipo and wife Giuseppina moved to Lodi, New Jersey where Philipo set up a Shoemaker Shop on Main Street in Lodi. At the time and for many years to follow, Lodi was a major Italian enclave of New Jersey and the New York Metro area on a whole. I once asked my Uncle Frank a few years back, what was the percentage of Italians in Lodi when he was growing up, and he told me without batting an eye, "100 %" all Italian. Yes Lodi was Italian, and these Italian immigrants were like my mother's parents Giuseppina & Philipo, from Sicily or Naples and its environs like; Benevento, Avellino, or Salerno where Uncle Franks better-half Aunt Helen was born.

Yes, I never met my grandparents on my mother's side of the family, Philipo and Giuseppina Bellino from Lercara Friddi Sicily. Nonna Giuseppina's maiden name was Salemi before marrying Philipo. My grandfather Philipo was a shoemaker from that town, and also, by the way, we have in common with one guy by the name of Francis Albert Sinatra, that his grandfather was a shoemaker from Lercara Friddi as well. Sinatra's father, Severio Antonio Martino Sinatra immigrated to America with his mother and two sisters in 1903, just one year before my grandparents. You can be pretty sure that in a small town like Lercari Friddi, that the Bellino and Sinatra families knew each other, especially as they were both from shoemaking families. Yes Francis Albert Sinatra, a.k.a. Frank Sinatra, or simply *Frank*, his father came from Lercara Friddi. And by the way, as we are talking of famous people from this town, there was another famous (infamous) Italian to come from the town of Lercara Friddi, Siciliy to settle in the Lower East Side of Manhattan, a guy by the name of Charles "Lucky" Luciano. Yes *Lucky*, the *Sinatra's*, and the *Bellino's* were just a few of many families to leave Italy (Sicilia), for a better life in America. Well my grandparents never got rich. You might say they were always poor. But being poor in America, was at the time, much better than being poor in Sicily and other parts of Southern Italy, like; Campania, Apulia, Calabria, Genoa, and Abruzzo. Back then, the poor of Italy were lucky to eat meat, maybe once a month or so, and chicken just two or three times a year. In America, maybe they'd have meat 2 or 3 times a week, or more. Things were a little better, even if you were poor. Most, sooner or later you would rise and make it to the middle class and a much better life, which in comparison to being poor in Italy, being middle class in America was actually almost like being rich. That was America back then.

Anyway, I never got to meet either of my mother's parents, as unfortunately they had both passed away by the time I was born. However, my grandmother Giuseppina would *live-on in her food* and recipes that she taught to my Mom, Uncle Tony, and Aunt Lilly, and how to cook the *Sicilian dishes* she learned to cook from her mother my maternal great grandmother, *name unknown*. Well, as of this date (March 3 2015) my great grandmother's name is unknown to us. I say as of now, as hopefully that will be changing soon. My cousin Tony and I are planning an ancestral trip to Sicily & Lercara Friddi this Summer. We will go to the town hall and the hall of records, and church where they were baptized, and try to get records and all the info we can on our ancestors the Bellino's & Salemi's of Lercara Friddi. And who knows, maybe my idol Francis Albert Sinatra is somehow related to us, or even the infamous *gangster* Charles *Lucky* Luciano. Who knows? Anyway, I'm oh so proud to be of Italian and of Sicilian heritage, and that my family even comes from the same town as the Greatest Italian-American of them all, Francis Albert Sinatra, and that both of our grandfathers were shoemakers from the same Sicilian town, yes you know it by now, it's Lercara Friddi, Sicilia.

So now back to my mother and her cooking and the recipes she learned from her mother Giuseppina. Sicilian recipes, and local recipes from Lercara Friddi & surrounding towns and cities like; Palermo, Corleone, Sciacca, Polizzi Generosa, Prizzi, and more.

I'd eat my mother's food, I'd watch her cook the dishes that her mother Giuseppina cooked for her, and also taught her to cook as well. Dishes like; Stuffed Peppers, Stuffed Artichokes, Eggplant Pamigiano, Pasta Lenticchie, Spaghetti Meatballs, Pasta Ceci, timballo, Zuppa di Cucuzza, Braciole, and many more. My grandmother taught them to my mother, and my mother Lucia taught them to my sister Barbara and I as well. Thus follows these, the Collected Recipes of my Grandmother, Giuseppina Salemi Bellino.

Daniel Bellino Z

SUNDAYS at THE BELLINO HOUSE

Sundays were always a special day at the Bellino House. Not just a special day but the best day of the week. Sunday was the day we'd go to my Aunt Fran and Uncle Tony Bellino's house in Lodi for a visit and Sunday Dinner. As most might know, Sunday Dinners in Italian-American households are no small thing. Sunday Dinner is an all day event, and in fact is not just a dinner, but a *Feast.*

Sunday at the Bellino House in Lodi was special. We'd (Me, Mommy, Jimmy, Bazzy, & Michael) head up to Lodi, always in great anticipation. We lived in East Rutherford, a few towns south, but my mother's brothers Tony and Jimmy had homes in Lodi a couple blocks from each other, and my mothers sister Lilly was right there too, with a house on Hunter Street, just feet from Aunt Fran and Uncle Tony's on Grove Street. Some of the meals we'd have at Aunt Helen and Uncle Frank's place in Hackensack, but more often than not they were at Aunt Wanda & Uncle Jimmy's on James Street, or over at Uncle Tony's house on Grove.

So we'd get to Aunt Fran's place and we'd walk up to the front door and ring the bell. Uncle Tony would answer the door and let us in. Everyone would be sitting around the kitchen table and I'd go around and say hello and *kiss* and get a *hug* from each and everyone of my aunts, uncles, and cousins. Then we'd settle in. Some times we'd arrive early and have some of Uncle Tony's Pepper and Egg

Sandwiches for breakfast, which was always a tasty treat. If we were at Aunt Helen's house over in Hackensack, those sandwiches would be made a bit different. Aunt Helen made me a sandwich that I will never forget, nor will any of my friends who've ever had the pleasure of tasting one. This sandwich is what I call *"The Aunt Helen Special."* Aunt Helen didn't have a name for it, so I gave it one, yes the Aunt Helen Special. Aunt Helen just called it an egg sandwich, and it was made with spinach sautéed with olive oil, a bit of butter and grated Parmigiano Reggiano, and put on a roll. It may not sound like much, but trust me, these simple ingredients, when made properly as Aunt Helen always did, taste more than supremely delicious, and as good as anything you will ever eat in your life. I kid you not.

Anyway, back to our Sundays. So, if we were lucky and arrived early in the morning, we'd have an egg sandwich from Tony or Helen. Uncle Tony's were with Peppers & Egg. This started our day off quite nicely. The Gravy (Sunday Sauce) if we were having one that day, would already be simmering away on the back of the stove. Yes the Sunday Sauce (Gravy) would be slowly cooking away. It was laden with Braciole and Sausages, and in the last 45 minutes of cooking, the meatballs would be thrown in. As the Sauce was simmering, we'd usually at some point, grab the loaf of bread, rip off a piece, dip it into the Gravy and eat it. It's a tradition *that must be done.* Remember Sonny Corleone in the Godfather? His mother was making some *Sauce,* Sonny walked in the kitchen, grabs some bread and dips it in the Sauce (Gravy). We always did the same. All Italian do! It's our *ritual*.

Anyway, we have an egg sandwich which holds us over until we sit down and start eating the main meal. After the egg sandwiches, the adults would sit down for Espresso, while we kids went outside and played. We'd get a few cookies and would be on our way until we sat down for Sunday Dinner.

Once it was dinnertime, we'd start with either a basic salad of Iceberg Lettuce with Cucumbers and Tomatoes dressed in Italian Olive Oil and Red Wine Vinegar. If we didn't have this salad, we might be having the more elaborate Antipasto. The antipasto was what millions of other Italian-American families would eat all over America as well. The mixed antipasto always had; Salami and Cheese, which would be either Provolone or Mozzarella or both. There was usually Sicilian Olives, Roast Red Peppers, and sticks of fresh Celery, and that was our antipasto and first course. Once in a while Aunt Fran would make Caponatina to eat on its own or as part of an antipasti misti.

After the first course of either; soup, salad, or some sort of antipasto, it was on to the main course, or as they say in Italy, Secondi. Sometimes Uncle Tony would make a Roast Pork or Roast Beef, or his famous Veal Marsala (my favorite). Also, we might have; Chicken Cacciatore, Lasagna, Lamb, or Roast Chicken, but most often it would be Gravy with Sausages Meatballs, and maybe Braciole, and of course this dish, also known as *Sunday Sauce* was always our favorite. There is nothing as wonderful as eating a Sunday Sauce on Sunday. Usually the Sunday Sauce, a.k.a. *Gravy* was served with a short maccheroni, either; Ziti or Rigatoni. The Sunday Sauce Gravy was always our favorite. Sometimes we'd have a Sunday Sauce, and we'd have some Ravioli after the antipasto course. Aunt Helen would take some sauce from the Gravy Pot and dress the Raviolis with it. Then we'd have the Braciole, the Sausages, and Meatballs served with potatoes and sauce.

After the Sunday Sauce or whatever main course it might have been, there was still a big part of the meal to go. This course was, as far as time is concerned, the biggest course of all, as once the grownups sat down for coffee, they'd be at the table for 3 or 4 hours or more to go, they'd be drinking coffee with all sorts of pastries like; Cannoli, Sfogiatelle, and more, including an assortment of Italian Cookies and quite possibly a Cheesecake or other homemade cake by Aunt Wanda or Helen. I always loved when aunt Fran made her Ricotta Cookies, or if Aunt Helen made Ciudatti (Sicilian Fig Cookies). The dessert course would last for hours, with all the grownups talking and the kids playing some game or another. But we'd frequently return to the table for another Cannoli and a couple more cookies. An Italian-American Sunday Dinner, I tell you, "there's nothing better."

Grandma Bellino's Italian Cookbook

ANTIPASTI

Antipasti? Many may know the antipasto course as the first course of an Italian meal, that's followed by a soup or pasta course (Primi), then the main course (Secondi), and finally Dolci, the dessert course. In our house, with my mother cooking, it wasn't that often we'd have an antipasto. Most often we'd have whatever the main course was, and nothing preceding it other than maybe a salad.
Though there were times we did, and that would usually be either Caponata or one of my moms truly favorites, stuffed Artichokes, which she'd make at least twice a month during the artichoke growing season. Yes there were other antipasti items, like; Stuffed Mushrooms, Clams Posillipo, Antipasti Misti, but these were usually reserved for dinner parties when company was coming over. When it came to items like baked Clams Oreganata, Clams Casino, Fried Calamari, Polpo alla Griglia, and the like, they were usually eaten in restaurants.

So, in a Nut Shell, when it comes to antipasto, we do love it, and much so. But when it came to nonna and my mother cooking, your everyday meal was more or less consisting of one course, the main course, whether it was; chicken, fish, meat, pasta, or soup, your meal was just the main course, sometimes you might have a salad, and if you were lucky, you'd get some sweets after dinner, and this is how it is for almost any family.

Although at dinner time when my mother and her siblings were growing up, most dinners were of just one course, the same as most American households, and the dinner was most often either soup or pasta, and occasionally a special sweet treat after dinner, this is not to say that antipasto items were not made by my grandmother or my mother. Antipasto dishes like Stuffed Artichokes, Caponata, Arancini, and Stuffed Peppers were made all the time, just not every night, but sometimes on Sundays and special occasion meals. Also, quite often many of these antipasto items would be made and eaten as a light lunch or even at dinner, especially items like Stuffed Artichokes, Rice Balls (Arancini), Polpettini (Meatballs), and Involtini di Peperoni. And in my grandmothers house and most Sicilians for that matter, Caponatina was always on hand and could be eaten on its own or as a light meal served with anything else like; a wedge of Frittata, Salami & Provolone, sautéed greens or a tossed salad. That's antipasto as it goes in our family, the Bellino's. And that's how antipasto was for most other Italian-American families in America as well. Basta!

CAPONATINA

This is my Nonna Giuseppina's recipe for one of Sicily's most iconic dishes, and without question, the # 1 Sicilian Antipasto item of them all, while Arancini (Sicilian Rice Balls) are neck-and-neck w/ Eggplant Caponata as far as popularity goes, and only Pasta con Sarde and Cannoli's would be more popular. Eggplant Caponata is a great antipasto item on its own, as part of a mixed antipasti, or served as an accompaniment on the plate of any fish, meat, or poultry dish at all. If you learn how to make it really well, you might even get famous in your circles for making it. Caponatina makes a wonderful gift presented in a nice glass Mason Jar, and anyone you give it to would be most happy to receive it.

Grandma Bellino's Italian Cookbook

RECIPE:

2 large eggplants, washed and cut into ¾" cubes, do not remove skin from Eggplant
½ cup olive oil
3 medium onions, cut into ¼" dice
1 small Red Pepper and 1 Yellow Pepper Cut into ½" dice
2 Celery stalks, ¼" dice
¼ raisons, soaked in hot water for 15 minutes
1 ½ cups Tomato Sauce
6 tablespoons sugar
6 tablespoons Balsamic vinegar
2 teaspoons salt, 3 teaspoons black pepper
3 tablespoons of capers

Sauté the peppers in a large pot with ½ of the olive oil for 10 minutes

Add the onions and sauté over low heat for 15 minutes.

Add the celery and tomato sauce and continue simmering. While the other ingredients are simmering, brown the Eggplant in several batches in a large frying pan with remaining olive oil. Add the browned Eggplant, sugar, and vinegar to the pot and simmer for 20 minutes over very low heat. Cool and serve on its own, as a topping for Crostini, as part of an Antipasto Misto, or as an accompaniment to any Grilled or Roast Fish, with Lamb, or with Grilled Chicken.

INVOLTINI di PEPERONI al NONNA
Grandma's Sicilian Stuffed Peppers

These Sicilian Stuffed Peppers are super tasty. Making stuffed peppers in this manner isn't very familiar to most Americans, or even Italian-Americans for that matter. This is my grandma's recipe that she passed down to my mother. The dish is very Sicilian and oh-so-tasty. Try it some time, and serve it to your friends. They'll love it!

RECIPE :

3 Red Bell Peppers & 3 Yellow Peppers
1 cup Italian Flavored Breadcrumbs
1 cup Provolone or Caciocavallo Cheese, diced
½ cup grated Pecorino Romano Cheese
1 small Egg
1 cup Gold Raisons
¼ cup Pine Nuts (optional)
8 tablespoons Olive Oil
Salt & Black Pepper

Cut each pepper in half from top to bottom. Pull out and discard the stems, seeds, and inner pith.

Add all remaining ingredients into a large glass or ceramic bowl. Mix well. This stuffing should be slightly moist. Not dry or water, but slightly moist.

Fill all the pepper halves with equal portions of the breadcrumb mixture.
Line a baking dish that will be large enough to hold all the peppers with olive oil.

Cook at 350 degrees for 30 to 35 minutes, until the skins begin to brown and the peppers are getting a bit soft, yet still a bit firm at the same time.

Remove from oven and let cool a few minutes. May be served warm, hot, or cold.

When serving, serve two per person. Sprinkle a bit of good Sicilian or other Olive Oil over the peppers and garnish with a nice basil flower or sprig of Italian Parsley if you have some. Serve hot or at room temperature.

NOTE: Two of these make a nice antipasto for 1 person, or 2 or 3 placed on a plate with a salad makes a nice light lunch or dinner. Enjoy!

ARANCINI

"SICILIAN RICE BALLS"

The Italian word for Aracine (Arancini) derives from the word orange, which many may not realize that these wonderful Sicilian Rice Balls resemble, as a result of being round with a skin on the outside and the flesh which is the rice that is flavored and colored with Saffron that gives the rice its orange-yellow tint that looks like the flesh of the inside of an orange. Arancini (Rice Balls) are one of Italy's and Italian-America's most iconic of dishes. In the world of Italian-America you will find these Rice Balls at; Italian Delis, in Pizzerias, restaurants, and homes all over the land. Though in Italy they are found all over the south, especially in Naples, Capri, and the Amalfi Coast, Aracini originated in Sicily and are often served in Wine Bars, Sicilian Caffes, Trattorias, Friggitorias, Foccacerias, and Salumerias. In Sicily, the inside of the Arancini are most often filled with a meat ragu, cheese, and peas. You might find them filled with meat ragu in Napoli & Campania as well, but more than not, in Campania they are usually filled with Mozzarella from the region and are called Suppli alla Telephono, as when they are bitten into, the fresh mozzarella stretches like a telephone wire. These Sicilian Rice Balls make a wonderful antipasto item and are great for snacks, or in a picnic-basket w/ Salami & Cheese and a nice bottle of Sicilian Wine. Enjoy!

RECIPE:

The FILLING

½ pound Ground Beef
3 tablespoons Olive Oil
1 small Onion, peeled and minced fine
½ cup Tomato Sauce (optional)
Salt & Black Pepper to taste
3/4 cup Frozen Peas

RICE :

1 pound Arborio Rice
4 cups Chicken Broth or water
1 small pinch Saffron
2 tablespoons Butter
½ cup grated Parmigiano Reggiano
1 extra Large Egg
Salt & White Pepper to taste
½ pound of Provolone or Cacciocavalo Chesse, cut into small chunks

BREADING

½ cup Flour
2 beaten Eggs
2 ½ cups Plain Breadcrumbs
4 cups Canola Oil for frying

Place the ground beef and onions in a pan with the Olive Oil and cook on a low flame until beef is cooked through, about 12 minutes. Season with salt and black pepper, about 1/ teaspoon each, or to your taste. Add peas and cook for 2 minutes. Turn heat off, and set aside to cool.

Add Chicken Broth (or Water if using) to a 6 quart pot with the rice, butter and ½ teaspoon salt. Bring liquid to the boil and stir as you do this. Once the liquid comes to the boil, turn heat to lowest flame possible and let cook without stirring for 16 minutes. Turn heat off and let rice set in the pot for 12 minutes.

Place the rice in a large glass bowl and let cool for 15 minutes.

Once the rice is completely cool, add ½ teaspoon white pepper and a ½ teaspoon of salt and the grated Parmigiano and mix. Add 1 beaten Egg and mix.

Take a handful of rice and place between both your hands and roll into balls that are just slightly smaller than a baseball, or you can make smaller if you like. Once you have shaped the rice into a ball, hold the rice ball with your left hand and push the thumb of your right hand into the ball to make a hole that goes to the center of the ball, making a hole that you will put the beef filling into.

Take about a tablespoon of the beef filling and put it into the hole. Place 1 or 2 pieces of the Provolone into the hole. Press rice around the hole to cover it up, and then round the rice between your two hands again to make the Rice Ball into a perfect ball shape. Continue this process until all the rice is gone and made into Rice Balls.

Get 3 small shallow bowls and put the flour in 1 bowl, the breadcrumbs in another bowl, and the beaten eggs into the 3rd bowl. Take a rice ball and put it into the bowl with the flour and gently roll it around until it is completely covered with a light coating of flour. Gently shake off any excess flour.

Now place the ball into the eggs and completely cover with the egg. Gently shake off any excess egg.

Now roll the rice ball with the egg on it into the breadcrumbs until ball is completely covered with breadcrumbs. Shake off excess. Repeat these last 3 steps with each rice ball until they are all coated with breadcrumbs.

Place the canola oil (or any vegetable oil) in a medium sized frying pan and heat to high. Fry a few rice balls at a time until golden brown. Fry all the rice balls and place on paper towels and let cool a few minutes before serving, at which point they will still be hot, but not too hot. Or you can let them cool further and serve at room temperature with or without Marinara Sauce on the side.

CARCIOFI REPIENO al SICILIANA
Sicilian Stuffed Artichokes

Stuffed Artichokes, scary looking, some have said. No I say, *"they are a thing of beauty."* In our Italian-American Cuisine, and among the Italian-American Community, the Stuffed Artichoke is a prized dish and one that is highly cherished. Yes, the Stuffed Artichoke is quite an awesome dish. Growing up in New Jersey and New York, these Carciofi Repieno were a popular item in our house, and we always loved eating them, as a fascinating little ritual that only an Italian Stuffed Artichoke could provide. You see there are certain steps to the process.

Yes, there it is, stuffed by mommy with a breadcrumbs, cheese, garlic, & herb mixture that taste oh-so-good. The Stuffed Artichoke, along with Eggplant Parmigiano, and Stuffed Shells were one of my mother's best dishes. As a young child watching my mother make the bread stuffing for the artichokes, stuffing them and cooking them was quite an experience. There is nothing quite like a Stuffed Artichoke in The World of Food. And more specifically, a Sicilian Stuffed Artichoke at that!

My mother would get her green mixing bowl, put in some Progresso Seasoned Breadcrumbs with Pecorino Cheese, a bit of Olive Oil, fresh chopped Garlic, and a bit of water. She mixed everything up with her hands, then took this savory breadcrumb mixture and stuffed every little crevice in that crazy looking vegetable with them.

My mother would put some chicken broth, Olive Oil, garlic and water in the bottom of a baking pan and put the artichokes in the oven. She'd cover the pan with aluminum foil and bake the artichokes until they were done.

Yes I used to watch my mother do this, along with stuffing and tying up the Beef Braciole one by one. I watched with amazement and curiosity, all these things always had great interest for me.

And oh when those artichokes were ready, "man oh man, we were happy as can be." I always remember, not having my own, but sharing one with my mom, and pulling the leaves off, and scraping the pulp on the leaves between my top row of teeth and the bottom ones. You bit down on the artichoke leaf and pulled it from back to front, scraping the pulp off the leaf and into your mouth. Yes that's how you do it. For all you Italians out there, *you know what I'm talking about.* For many of you, this may all sound very strange, and all I can tell you, that if you've never eaten a Sicilian Style Stuffed Artichokes, you don't know what you're missing, and you just gotta try them one day. And if this all sounds strange to you, and you're saying, "What the Hell is he talking about?" Again, you have to just trust me on this and try them, I guarantee, you'll be glad you do.

RECIPE : STUFFED ARTICHOKES

Ingredients:

4 large, full-size artichokes
1 lemon, halved
1 3/4 cups dried breadcrumbs
1 cup grated pecorino
1/3 cup chopped flat-leaf parsley leaves
2 tsp. kosher salt
1 tsp. freshly ground black pepper
8 cloves garlic, finely chopped
5 tbsp. extra-virgin olive oil

Using a serrated knife, cut off artichoke stems to create a flat bottom. Cut top thirds off artichokes, pull off tough outermost leaves, and trim tips of leaves with kitchen shears. Rub cut parts with lemon halves. Open artichoke leaves with your thumbs to make room for stuffing; set aside.

Heat oven to 350°. In a large bowl, combine breadcrumbs, 3/4 cup pecorino, parsley, salt, pepper, and garlic. Working with one artichoke at a time over bowl, sprinkle one-quarter of breadcrumb mixture over the artichoke and work it in between leaves.

Transfer stuffed artichoke to a shallow baking dish. Drizzle each artichoke with 1-tablespoon oil. Pour in boiling water to a depth of 1".. Cover pan and artichokes with foil.

Bake Artichokes until a knife easily slides into the base of an artichoke, about 35- 40 minutes. Remove foil, sprinkle tops with remaining cheese. Turn heat up to 400 degrees and bake for 10 minutes more.

SERVES 4

MELANZANE BECCAFICIO
Eggplant Beccaficio

Italians eat eggplant all over Italy, but mostly in the south. Northern Italians hardly don't eat it that much, while in Tuscany and Central Italy they like eggplant a lot more than northerners do. When we talk about eggplant and the south of Italy, it's hugely popular, especially in Campania and its capital city Napoli. But nowhere in Italy is eggplant eaten and revered more than in Sicily. And Sicilians make many more different eggplant dishes than any other region do. Dishes like their hugely famous Eggplant Caponata, Pasta alla Norma (w/ eggplant & tomato) Eggplant Parmigiano, and this dish Melanzane Beccafico. And as far as Italian eggplant dishes in America, Epplant Parmigiano has been very popular with Americans for some 100 years or so, however, before the end of the last century, very few Americans outside of those of Italian ancestry ever ate or knew what Eggplant Caponata was, and have only discovered it in recent years, and there are still many Americans who still have never heard of the dish at all. Now this dish, Eggplant Beccafico is very rare when it comes to Americans. Very few of the total mass of Italian-Americans even know of the dish, and it's not even that well known among a good number of Sicilian Americans as well. Do you get what I'm getting at? Melanzane Beccafico is not well known in this country. I love the dish which I discovered in Sicily 25 years ago and have eaten it ever since. And to tell you the truth, when I had my restaurant/ wine bar Bar Cichetti back in the 90's, and served it there, I had never seen it served in any Italian restaurant in America before that time, and even still to this day.

There's also a dish called Sarde al Beccafico, that's made with the same breadcrumb stuffing that you put inside the eggplant beccafico. Both dishes are wonderful, very unique, and oh so tasty. The recipe follows below. Make it, and surprise your friends and family with it, of whom I'm sure, most will have never had it before.

RECIPE:

3 Small Eggplants, washed
1 ½ cups Tomato Sauce

Breadcrumb Stuffing :

¼ cup Olive Oil
1 medium Onion, peeled and minced fine
2 cloves Garlic, peeled and minced fine
3 Anchovy Filets, minced fine
¼ cup fresh Parsley, chopped
1 – ¼ cup plain dry Breadcrumbs
4 tablespoons Golden Currants
5 tablespoons Pignoli Nuts, toasted
2 ounce Provolone, cut into very small pieces
1/2 tablespoons grated Pecorino Romano Cheese

Place currants in hot water, and soak for 15 minutes to get soft. Drain and set aside.

Cut the eggplants lengthwise into 1/8 " slices. If you don't have a Madeline type implement to do this, maybe you can get your local deli to slice the eggplant for you on their slicer machine.

Coat a cookie sheet with the Eggplant slice. Cook in a 400 degrees oven for 8-10 minutes. Remove from oven and let cool.

Add Olive Oil and onions to a large frying pan and cook on medium heat for 5 minutes. Add minced Anchovies and cook 2 minutes on medium heat.

Add Garlic and cook on low heart for 2 minutes.

Add breadcrumbs and cook until bread gets lightly golden in color. Remove from heat and let cool for 15 minutes.

Add Provolone, Parsley, Currants, half the grated Pecorino Cheese, and Pignoli Nuts and mix.

Place a slice of the roasted eggplant down and place about 3 tablespoons of breadcrumb mixture on one end of the eggplant. Roll eggplant up into a roll, and place down on a cookie sheet that has been coated with olive oil. Repeat until all the eggplant slices are rolled-up and filled breadcrumb mixture.

Spoon a bit of tomato sauce over each rolled-up piece of eggplant and sprinkle with a little grated Pecorino each, making sure to reserve some tomato sauce to put on plate later.

Bake Eggplant in a 350 degree oven until heated through. About 12 minutes.

Serve this as an antipasto on its own or as part of an Antipasti Misti (mixed Antipasto). If serving as an antipasto on its own, place a little tomato sauce down on a plate, then place 2 or 3 pieces of eggplant on each plate. Drizzle with a little Olive Oil and chopped Parsley or Basil Leaf if you have it. Sprinkle on a bit more Pecorino and serve.

MELANZANE SOTTO' OLIO
Eggplant Preserved in Oil

My grandmother would make large batches of these preserved eggplants, along with canning tomatoes, preserving Roast Peppers, and other vegetables from her small garden in the summer and fall months each year as a way to save money and have ready vegetables from the families garden long after the hot Summer Months had pasted. By doing so, she could pull a few Eggplant Slices, along with her preserved Roast Red Peppers, and serve an Antipasti Misti with a few slices of Salami and Provolone, and the family or any company that was visiting her house would have something to eat at a moments notice, any day of the week, anytime of the day.

If company was over, she could serve one of these lovely antipasto plates to her guest, and if they needed a more substantial meal, a plate of Spaghetti Pomodoro or other pasta dish could always be made in no-time-flat!

INGREDIENTS :

6 small Eggplants, peeled
2 cups White Distilled Vinegar
Several Bay Leaves
Sea Salt & whole Black Peppercorns
Pepperoncino (Red Pepper flakes)
Canola Oil
Olive Oil
Red Wine Vinegar

Place vinegar and 3 quarts of water in a large non-corrosive pot with 4 tablespoons of Sea Salt. Bring to the boil and let boil a few minutes.

Slice the Eggplants long-ways into ¼" slices. Place eggplant slices in the boiling water and cook at the boil for 3 minutes. Remove eggplants and drain in a colander. Dry all the eggplant slices with a towel.

Place 1 teaspoons of Sea Salt, 2 tablespoons of Red Wine Vinegar, 1 Bay Leaf, a pinch of Oregano, and 1 teaspoon Peppercorns, and a half-teaspoon of red pepper flakes (Pepperoncini), in each Mason Jar.

Place eggplant slices in Mason Jars to fill. Fill each Mason Jar half way with Canola Oil. Add Olive Oil to come to 2" below the top of each jar. Screw lids on each jar and shake to mix contents. Open Jars, and fill the jars with Olive Oil. Screw lids tightly on each jar and store in a cool dark place for up to 2 months.

INSALTA di POLPO
Octopus Salad

Along with Tuna, Swordfish, Sardines, and Mussels, Octopus is one of Sicily's utmost favorite of seafood items. If you like, use the preparation here for cooking the octopus, and you can make Octopus Salad, or at the point where the Octopus is finished cooking you can serve it hot as Bolito di Polpo, along with boiled potatoes or some sautéed Broccoli Rabe or other vegetable as you like it. We love our Polpo, and if you make it either of these two ways, boiled and served hot or as the Octopus Salad, you're sure to love it too! Buon Appetito!

RECIPE :

1 – Frozen Octopus about 2 pounds washed
1 Bay Leaf
2 or 3 Corks
¼ cup Olive Oil
2 large Potatoes, boiled until tender
2 stalks Celery, washed and cut to ½" pieces
Juice of 1 Lemon
1 tablespoon Red Wine Vinegar
½ teaspoon each of Sea Salt & Black Pepper
¼ teaspoon Red Pepper flakes (optional)
¼ cup Fresh Parsley, washed, dried, and chopped

Place the Octopus in a large pot with Bay Leaf and Corks if you have the. Cover the octopus with water and bring to the boil, then immediately lower heat so the octopus is cooking at a gentle simmer. Let cook for 1 hour, uncovered. Take lid off and let the octopus sit in the hot water. After 30 minutes, remove octopus from the water and drain in a colander. Shake off excess water and let the octopus rest in the colander for 30 minutes.

Cut the potatoes into 1" cubes. When the octopus is cooking, cook the potatoes in boiling salted water until just slightly tender, about 6 minutes.

Drain the potatoes and let cool.

Cut the Octopus into 1 /2 inch pieces and put in a large glass or ceramic bowl with the potatoes. Add all the remaining ingredients and mix.

Your Insalata di Polpo is ready to serve. Serve as an antipasto, as part of a mixed antipasto or as a main course if you like.

CLAMS POSILLIPO

Clams Posillipo, is a great favorite of almost every Italian-American, especially here in New York, and in its birthplace of course, the beautiful city by the bay, la Bella Napoli. Sicilian-Americans love it as well, like my cousin Tony and my brother Michael, as well as every Sicilian I know.

RECIPE :

3 dozen Littleneck Clams or 3 lbs.
or Cockles or Manila Clams
1 ½ cups Tomato Sauce
½ teaspoon Red Pepper flakes
½ cup dry White Wine
7 cloves of garlic, peeled and sliced
1 ½ cups water
3 tablespoons fresh Parsley, roughly chopped
Olive Oil

Put wine into a large pot and turn flame on to high. Cook and reduce the wine to half of its original volume.

Add water, garlic, Red Pepper, and tomato sauce. Bring to boil. Lower to a simmer and let cook three minutes.

Add Clams to pot. Turn heat up to high. Cover pot. Cook and watch when clams have opened. Once the clams have opened, lower heat to medium. Remove cover. Mix clams with a large spoon while cooking for 1 ½ minutes. Turn flame off. Add Parsley and mix. Portion out into bowls, with equal portions of Clams and broth for each person. Serve with toasted Italian Bread.

FUNGHI REPIENO
Stuffed Mushrooms

Sicilians are famous for making dishes with seasoned breadcrumbs, a result of many years of their extreme poverty and frugalness, yet these dishes are super-tasty never-the-less, you're sure to agree, and as Stuffed Mushrooms have long been a favorite party item of Italian Weddings and for other family get-together's as well. These stuffed mushrooms are sure to please. Enjoy them as we always do.

RECIPE:

24 medium sized domestic Button Mushrooms
1 small Onion, peeled and minced
6 tablespoons Olive Oil, Tbs. butter
¼ cup Italian-Style Breadcrumbs
¼ cup grated Parmigiano Reggiano Cheese
Salt & Pepper to taste
¼ cup fresh chopped Italian Parsley

Brush off and remove any dirt that might be on the mushrooms and clean well. Break off mushroom stems and chop fine. Place Olive Oil, butter, onions, and chopped mushroom stems in a large frying pan and cook over low heat for about 7 minutes until mushrooms and onions are cooked through. Set aside and let cool.

Add the breadcrumbs to pan with the cooled mushrooms and mix. Add all remaining ingredients and mix well. The mixture should be just slightly moist. If its not, you can add a little bit more olive oil or a little water just to moisten the mixture a little.

Fill each Mushroom Cap with the breadcrumb mushroom mixture so there is a little heaping dome on the each mushroom cap.

Heat the oven to 375 degrees. Place all the mushrooms in a baking pan with a thin film of olive oil on bottom of pan. Bake mushrooms for about 15 minutes until the mushrooms are cooked through. Serve and enjoy.

FUNGHI REPIENO con SALSICCIA
SAUSAGE STUFFED MUSHROOMS

A bit different from the previous Stuffed Mushroom recipe, they're both very good. I prefer the previous recipe, but many like this one better, so I've included it here. Uncle Tony likes this one, as he loves his Sausage and often brought some home from his friends, at the Scarlotta's Butcher Shop where he worked as a teenager growing up in Lodi, New Jersey ..

INGREDIENTS:

24 medium sized domestic Button Mushrooms
2 links of Italian Sweet Sausage, skin removed and sausage broken up
1 medium Onion, peeled and minced fine
¼ cup Italian Parsley, washed, dried, and chopped
¼ pound Provolone, cut into small chunks
¼ cup, plain dry Breadcrumbs
3 tablespoons Olive Oil
Salt & Black Pepper

Place the crumbled sausage meat in a frying pan with olive oil and cook on low heat for about 10 minutes until the sausage meat is cook through. Make sure to leave some of the oil behind in pan to cook the onions.

Remove the sausage meat with a slotted spoon and set aside in a large bowl to cool.
Remove stems from the mushrooms, chop and sauté with and cook with the onions.

Place the minced onions & mushroom stems in the pan with reserved oil from cooking the sausage and cook the onions on low heat for 10 minutes. Turn heat off, season onions with salt & black pepper to taste.

Once the sausage & onions have cooled down completely, add the Parsley, Provolone, and Breadcrumbs and mix well.

Fill each Mushroom Cap with some of the sausage mixture until all the caps are stuffed. Bake on a greased cookie sheet in a 375 degree oven for 15 minutes. Place on a plate and serve on a buffet table, or if serving as an antipasto, give each person four mushrooms garnished with a sprig of Parsley or Basil.

TORTINO di CARCIOFI e SPINACI
Spinach & Artichoke Tart

This is a nice dish that my grandmother used to make and serve as a main meal for a nice little lunch or light dinner-time meal. She would make it and cut a couple slices for my grandfather to bring to his shoemaker shop, so he would have a little something to snack on during the day. This Tortino is easy to make, and is actually a sort of a baked frittata, even though it's called *tortino*. It's great to make, eat some and save some to eat the next day if you wish. You can serve it as an antipasto, main-course, in a picnic basket, or as a tasty satisfying snack at any time of the day, a little wedge of it will do the trick.

RECIPE :

6 frozen Artichoke Bottom or Hearts, thawed
1 pound fresh Spinach, washed
1 small Onions peeled and minced fine
3 tablespoons Butter, 2 tablespoons Olive Oil
¼ teaspoon each of Salt & ground Black Pepper
10 extra large Eggs, beaten
¾ cup grated Caciocavallo or Parmigiano Cheese
½ cup dry Breadcrumbs

Grease a 9 or 10 inch round glass pie pan with one tablespoon of butter. Take the breadcrumbs and pour into pan and shake around until breadcrumbs are sticking to the butter throughout the pan. Discard excess crumbs. Set pan aside.

Slice artichoke bottoms into ¼ inch slices. Place remaining butter and Olive Oil in a large frying pan with the Artichoke bottoms. Cook over high heat for 4 minutes. And onions and cook on low heat for 2 minutes. Add half the Salt & Black Pepper and cook 2 minutes while stirring.

Add the spinach to pan and cook on high heat for 2 minutes while mixing with a wooden spoon. Lower heat to low and cook on low heat for 2 minutes while stirring. Turn heat off and let the contents cool for at least 20 minutes. After the spinach and artichokes have cooled, add to the beaten eggs with the grated cheese and mix with a wooden spoon.

Heat oven to 375 degrees. Place the contents of the eggs, artichokes and spinach into the pie pan. Bake in the oven at 350 degrees for 15 minutes. Turn heat down to 325 and cook until a toothpick put into the center of tortino comes out dry with no wet egg in it, about 20 minutes more for a total of approximately 35 minutes total cooking time.

Remove from oven. Let rest 7 minutes before serving. To serve as an antipasto, cut a small slice that is appropriate for an appetizer size, or cut a larger piece if serving as a main-course for lunch or a lite dinner along with a small green salad or Caponata on the side.

POLPETTINI AGRO DOLCE
Sweet & Sour Sicilian Meatballs

These are tasty little Sicilian Meatballs that are a bit different then the norm of being served with tomato sauce. Sicilians like to put raisons in their meatballs and sometimes Pignoli Nuts and serve them Agro Dolce in a Sweet & Sour Sauce as opposed to a Marinara Sauce. They are quite tasty and will make either a great Antipasto or tasty item for a Buffet Table. My mother used to make them for us every year at our New Years Eve Party at our house watching Guy Lombardo. She'd also make Deviled Eggs and crispy Celery Stuffed with Cream Cheese & Sweet Paprika. Oh, the good old days?

MEATBALLS :

1 pound ground Veal
¼ cup grated Pecorino Romano Cheese
1 small Onion, peeled and minced fine
¼ cup Plain Breadcrumbs
3 tablespoons Raisons
¼ cup Milk
½ cup fresh Parsley, washed, dried and chopped
½ teaspoon each Salt & Black Pepper
2 Eggs, beaten
½ cup Canola Oil or other vegetable oil

For The SAUCE :

¼ cup Sweet Marsala Wine
2 tablespoons Tomato Paste
1 ½ tablespoons Sugar
6 tablespoons Red Wine Vinegar
3 tablespoons Raisons
3 tablespoons toasted Pignoli Nuts (optional)
¼ cup water

Soak Raisons in hot water for 15 minutes to soften, then drain dry.

Place the breadcrumbs and milk in a large glass mixing bowl and let sit for 5 minutes. Add all remaining ingredients for the meatballs except for the canola oil to bowl and mix with your hands. When adding the Parsley, just add half and use the other half to garnish the meatballs once they are done.

Form the veal mixture into balls the size of Golf Balls until all the veal is used up.

Place oil in a medium size frying pan and turn heat on to high. Once oil is heat to hot place half the meatballs in and fry on all side, being careful they do not burn. Should be golden brown.

Once all the meatballs are nicely brown, set aside on a plate.

Discard oil from pan and add Marsala. Turn heat to high and cook the Marsala Wine until it reduced by half its original volume.

Add vinegar, raisons, Sugar, and Tomato Paste and cook on medium heat for 5 minutes.

Add the Meatballs to the pan with the sauce and cook on low heat until meatballs are cooked though in the center, about 10 minutes on low heat. Add half the remaining Parsley and mix.

If serving meatballs on a buffet table, put all the meatballs on a large platter with the sauce, and sprinkle with Pignoli Nuts and remaining chopped Parsley. Then stick each Meatball with a toothpick so guest can easily eat them.

If serving as an antipasto item during dinner, serve each person about 5 meatballs each with a little sauce on their plate, sprinkled with Parsley.

Grandma Bellino's Italian Cookbook

POLLO POMODORO
Stuffed Tomatoes

This dish makes a nice little antipasto, serve 1 per person as a starter, or serve two as a light lunch main course. This also makes a nice item on a buffet table as well.

INGREDIENTS:

8 medium Salad Tomatoes
1 cup Roast Peppers from a jar, drained and chopped
4 Scallions, washed and chopped
¼ cup Parsley, washed dried & chopped
3 Chicken Breasts, on the bone
¾ cup Mayonnaise
Salt & Black Pepper
8 leaves of Boston Lettuce
1 Lemon cut into 8 wedges

Place the chicken breast in a small pot and fill with water. Cook the chicken in low simmering water until cooked through, about 10 minutes. Turn heat off, and remove chicken to a bowl, and let cool for 12 minutes. After 12 minutes, remove the chicken meat from the bones, and discard the bones. Let the chicken keep cooling.

Slice the tops off the tomatoes and set aside. Scoop the inside core out of the tomatoes and discard. Place the tomatoes upside down on a plate to drain.

After the chicken has cooled, cut into ½" sized cubes and place in a mixing bowl. Add chopped Scallions and Parsley to bowl. Season the chicken with salt & black pepper to taste, and mix. Add mayonnaise and mix.

Fill each tomato with some of the chicken mixture until all the tomatoes are full.

To serve, place lettuce on the bottom of a plate, place one tomato in the middle of each plate and garnish with a lemon wedge.

INSALATA *"Salad"*

I've heard that the normal tossed salad wasn't all that popular with my grandmother. She was more apt to be serving Sautéed Escarole, Green Beans, Cauliflower Salad, Caponatina, Potatoes, Roast Peppers, Stufata di Cucuzza, or some other form of vegetable, rather than serving a tossed green salad.

INSALATA del NONNA

My mother would make this salad that's almost like a vegetable antipasto mixed all-together. She said her mother made it all the time, once or even two times a week, as she'd make a batch, serve it and keep it in the frig to eat for lunch the next day or two. My mother did the same, as do I. It's a great way of getting your vegetables, and the different colors look great on a plate. This salad is great as a first course antipasto or as the accompaniment to any piece of roast or grilled fish or chicken.

RECIPE: INSALTA di NONNA

1 ½ pounds Green Beans
1 cup Roast Red Peppers (fresh or from a jar)
1 head of Cauliflower
½ cup large Sicilian Green Olives
¼ cup Sicilian Olive Oil
4 tablespoons best quality Red Wine Vinegar

2 ripe Salad Tomatoes, washed and cut into 8 wedges each tomato
¼ Italian Parsley, washed, dried and chopped

Cut hard ends off of the green beans and blanch in boiling salted water for 4 minutes. Remove from heat to stop cooking and run under cold water for a couple minutes. Put in a colander and let all the water drain away.

Remove center core from the cauliflower and discard. Cut the cauliflower into 1 - 1/2" chunks. Cook in boiling salted water until just slightly tender, about 6 minutes. Drain in a colander.

Cut the roast pepper in chunks. Place the peppers and all the rest of the vegetable and the Olives in the large bowl. Do not put the tomatoes in. Only put a couple wedges of tomatoes on top of the salad at the time you serve it.
Add olive oil and vinegar and mix, season with Salt & Black Pepper, about one teaspoon of each. Mix salad well.

Serve this salad as an antipasto or salad course or alongside some grilled or roast fish, poultry, or meat. When serving, put a wedge or two on top of the salad. Store remaining salad in air-tight containers for up to 3 or 4 days.

Daniel Bellino Z

INSALTA di FAGIOLINI VERDE
Green Bean & Potato Salad

This salad is much like the previous one, except with less ingredients. It's wonderful just the same, and a bit quicker to put together.

Ingredients:

1 pound of Green Beans, cleaned and cooked the same as for the directions of cooking the green beans in the preceding recipe.
3 Idaho Potatoes
½ cup Roast Red Peppers from a jar
1/3 cup best quality Olive Oil
6 tablespoons good quality Red Wine Vinegar
1 teaspoon Sea Salt
½ teaspoon ground Black Pepper

Peel Potatoes, then cut in half lengthwise, then cut into ¼" half moon-looing slices. Boil the potatoes until just slightly tender, about 3 minutes. Remove from heat and strain in a colander. Let cool for 5 minutes, then place in a large ceramic or glass bowl with the olive oil. Mix potatoes gently with the olive oil.

Add all remaining ingredients. Mix completely and serve.

INSALATA di CECI .. *Chickpea Salad*

Chickpeas are another mainstay of the Sicilian Kitchen. They are most popular in the widespread Street Food of Palermo & Cantania and are a staple of many Foccacerias. You will find them in Panelle, Soups, and Pasta, or in salads as this one here. This salad is quick and easy to make, most Sicilians and Sicilian Americans would always have the items to make this dish in their pantry at all times.

2 cans Chickpeas, drained and washed
1 small Red Onion, peeled and minced
1 clove Garlic, peeled and minced
8 tablespoons Olive Oil
2 tablespoons imported Italian Red Wine Vinegar
¾ cup Green Olives
½ teaspoon each of Sea Salt & Black Pepper
¼ cup Roast Red Peppers from a jar (optional)
¼ cup chopped fresh Italian Parsley (optional)

The basic Insalata di Ceci as made in Sicily is made with all the ingredients here, minus the Roast Peppers and Parsley, which when you are making this salad, you can either use or omit. And if you like, you can add other ingredients like, fresh Green Beans, Cherry Tomatoes, Potatoes or whatever you like. It's up to you. To make the salad, place all the ingredients in a large glass or ceramic bowl and mix. That's it! It's as easy as that! Mangia Bene.

SECRET SALAD DRESSING - *CREAMY ITALIAN*

Use this tasty Secret Salad Dressing to make the most wonderful mixed salad of Lettuce & Tomatoes, and perhaps a few Cucumbers if you like, I know I do!

INGREDIENTS:

½ Cup Mayonnaise
¼ cup Olive Oil, ¼ Red Wine Vinegar
1 tablespoon water, 1 Garlic Clove, minced fine
¼ teaspoon each of Salt & Black Pepper
¼ teaspoon dry Oregano, ¼ teaspoon dry Basil

Place Mayonnaise and half the Olive Oil in a mixing bowl and mix with a wire-whip. Add remaining Olive Oil, mix again. Add vinegar a little at a time and mix.

Add all remaining ingredients and mix vigorously.

Place whatever lettuce you choose in a large bowl. Add Creamy Italian Dressing, mix and serve.

NOTE: You can make a salad with this tasty dressing with whatever lettuce and other ingredients you choose. Our favorite is Boston Bibb Lettuce with Cucumbers and Ripe Fresh Tomatoes, Iceberg or Romaine Lettuce also works well.

INSALATA SICILIANA

This is a salad that showcases a number of Sicily's favorite ingredients, like; Anchovies, Green Sicilian Olives, Tomatoes, Mussels, and preserved Tuna. This salad makes a great little lunch on its own, or may be served in smaller portions as an antipasto, or as a buffet-table item as well.

INGREDIENTS :

2 Idaho Potatoes, peeled cubed and boiled
½ cup Green Sicilian Olives, pits removed
3 tablespoons Red Wine Vinegar
3 Anchovy Filets, minced
¼ cup Olive Oil1 /12 cups Cherry Tomatoes
3 stalks Celery, washed and cut in 1" pieces
1/8 teaspoon each Salt, Black Pepper, Oregano
¼ cup chopped fresh Parsley
1 ½ Mussels, cleaned and steamed until opened
2 cans Italian Tuna (or Cento) drained of oil
2 ripe Salad Tomatoes, washed and cut in 6 pieces

Place mussels in a large pot with ¾ cup water. Cover pot and steam until all the mussels open. Discard any mussels that don't open. Set aside to cool.

Boil potatoes in salted water until slightly tender. Drain in colander and let cool.

Place; Olive Oil, Vinegar, Salt & Pepper, and Anchovies in a large glass bowl and mix. Add Potatoes & Olives and mix.

Remove Mussels and add to bowl with the chopped Parsley and Mix. Add Tomatoes.
Divide the Tuna among 4-6 plates, putting the tuna in the center of the plate. Surround the tuna with the Salad and serve.

INSALATA di TONNO
Sicilian Tuna & Bean Salad

Here's another salad that features a number of the favored Sicilian ingredients in its contents. These ingredients being Sicilian Capers from the Sicilian Island of Pantelleria, good Sicilian Olive Oil, fresh ripe Tomatoes, and the star of the show, Tuna caught off the shores of Sicily. This salad is quick and easy to make, and doesn't require any cooking at all, just a little chopping of the vegetables and mixing the ingredients together. This salad is often served as an antipasto in restaurants or in your home, and it makes a wonderful lunch (main course) served in a larger portion than for an antipasto, and perhaps with nice crusty Italian Bread and a crispy Sicilian White Wine as well. Buon Appetito!

RECIPE:

2 -7 ounce cans Italian Tuna, preferably Sicilian
2 cans Cannellini Beans, drained and washed
1/3 cup Sicilian Olive Oil (or any Italian Olive Oil)
4 tablespoons Red Wine Vinegar
Half a small Red Onion, cut into very thin slices
½ teaspoon each of Sea Salt & Black Pepper
1 Garlic Clove, peeled and minced fine (optional)
¼ cup fresh Italian Parsley, chopped
5 tablespoons Capers from Pantelleria (washed)
2 stalks of Celery, washed and cut to ¾" slices
1 cup and a half Cherry Tomatoes, cut in half
¼ cup Castelvetrano Olives
In a large glass or ceramic bowl, mix all of these ingredients except for the tuna (Tonno), Parsley, and and the Olives.

Add 2/3 of the Parsley and Olives and mix.

Remove the tuna from the can and break into 6 pieces per can. Add to salad with the tomatoes, and gently mix all with a wooden spoon.

If serving as an antipasto item, plate the salad among 4 to 6 plates. Sprinkle remaining parsley over top of each plate.

If serving as a main course, serve this amount of salad to 2 to 4 people, and if you like, you can add another can or two of tuna to this recipe.

Note: As we've already said, capers from the beautiful Sicilian Island of Pantelleria are considered the best in the world. If you get them, they are usually packed in salt, which needs to be washed off. If you can't get these capers use any that you get your hands on. For the tuna in this salad it is an absolute must to use Tuna packed in Olive Oil from Italy. We prefer Sicilian Tonno, but other Italian Tonno is just as good, especially the tonno that comes from Genoa and Liguria. The same goes for the Olive Oil.

PS ... Besides growing the world's best capers, the tiny island of Pantelleria produces one of the world's greatest dessert wines in Passito di Pantelleria. If you've never had it, get a bottle and treat your guest to it, the next time you have a dinner party.

Grandma Bellino's Italian Cookbook

INSALATA di CAVOLFIORE
Sicilian Cauliflower Salad

This is a healthy refreshing salad, made with one of Sicily's cherished ingredients, *cauliflower*. The dish is quite easy to make and is a great item to serve as a first course at a dinner party, as you can make it the day before or early in the day of your dinner or lunch party. A great second course at a dinner party to go along with this dish would be Timballo di Anelletti, or Sausage & Beans. Whatever you choose, it's sure to be good, so put this one in your repertoire and enjoy.

RECIPE :

1 head Cauliflower
¼ cup Olive Oil & 4 tablespoons Red Wine Vinegar
1 cup large Green Olives, pits removed
1 cup Roast Peppers, fresh roasted or from a jar
5 tablespoons Sicilian Capers
½ teaspoon each Sea Salt & Black Pepper
¼ cup chopped fresh Parsley
20 Cherry Tomatoes, washed and left whole
8 Anchovy Filets (optional)

Remove the discard the core from the head of Cauliflower. Cut the cauliflower into 1 ½" pieces and boil in rapidly boiling salted water until the cauliflower is tender yet slightly firm.
Remove from heat and drain the cauliflower in a colander. Let cool for 4 minutes.

Place the cauliflower in a large ceramic or glass serving bowl. Add all remaining ingredients and mix thoroughly. Let set at least 20 minutes before serving. As the salad is setting, mix once or twice so the salad gets to marinate completely.

Serve this salad on its own, as part of an antipasti misto, or on the side of grilled or roast fish, meat, or poultry.

NOTE : To the above recipe, you can add whatever other vegetables you like, such as, boiled potatoes, carrots, and or green beans. If you do add more vegetables, adjust the seasoning and add a bit more Olive Oil & Vinegar, Salt & Pepper.

Daniel Bellino Z

ZUPPE

Zuppa, Zuppe, Minestra, are all names for what we call soup. And when it comes to soup and what one considers a full Italian meal in a restorante in Italy, your full meal will start with an antipasto for the first course, followed by the Primi, the 2nd course, with primi meaning before the main course, and then Dolci, the dessert course. Soup falls into the primi category, which also includes Risotto & Pasta. When it comes to the Bellino Family, my grandmother, my mom, and most other people's mothers and grandmothers, if they were serving up soup in Italian-American households, it most likely would be 90% of the time served as a main course, not as a starter or primi, which is normally the second course, but the main and only course. Well maybe not only, as you might be getting dessert, and you might even get a salad beforehand, but one thing was usually for sure, if you are having soup in most Italian-American homes, it's usually the main course, whether for lunch, dinner, and even breakfast. Do you get my drift? So, actually, when my mother was growing up, soup was, as concerns *money, time, and ease of preparation,* thee # 1 most frequently served item most nights in the Bellino household by Nonna Giuaeppina was Soup. She made zuppa all the time, and by all the time, I'm talking almost everyday, either for; breakfast, lunch, or dinner, maybe even all 3 meals.

Soups at the Bellino house might include; Zuppa di Lenticchie (Lentils), Pasta Ceci, Pasta Fagioli, Minestrone (mixed Vegetables), Escarole & Beans, Chicken Soup, or Spit Pea. All these soups are easy to make. You make one big pot and get maybe 16 portions out of it, meaning that my grandma could serve her husband, herself, and 5 children at least 2 meal from the one pot, and if she doubled up the recipe, she'd get 4 full meals from the pot. Most any soup is quite cheap to make, you only use one pot, so there's less dishes to clean, and you make enough to get several meals from. Once you cook the soup, when you go to eat it again a couple days later, all you have to do is put the soup in a pot, turn the heat on, heat the soup, and you can eat it in just about 7 minutes. It's as easy as that. Most soups take just a little more than an hour to make, and once it's done and left in containers in the frig, you'll get a number of meals from the batch and it will just take you a few minutes to heat up. So besides being economical in a monetary (money) way, soups are the best item by far for what I like to call time-economics. You save money and you save time. I myself, for years, most of the time when I'm cooking food to eat at home, most often I'll make either soup, Tomato Sauce, a Stew of some sort, or my famed Ragu Bolognese. All these items, soups, stews, and certain sauces are all at the top of the chain of best dishes for saving time. You spend some time when you make a big pot of any of these items, you'll eat a meal when you're done cooking it, and then you'll have lots of leftovers for several meals to come. And the two greatest things about all these foodstuffs, is that they do not suffer from being stored in the refrigerator and being reheated. They taste just as good, and sometimes even better after they set a while, and # 2, they only take a few minutes to reheat to get all your subsequent meals from. "What's better than that?" Not much, I'd say. So yes, soups were, are now, and always will be, quite big in our family. They are for millions of Italian Americans, and they should be for you too.

All my Grandmother Giuseppina's soup recipes follow below. Make them, savor them, give them away to your friends and family, and just enjoy them. And as always, Mangia Bene!

ZUPPA di LENTICCHIE e SALSICCIA
Lentil Soup w/ Sausage

I love my Zuppa di Lenticchie, especially when I make it with some tasty Italian Sausages. As far as soups go, its my all-time favorite, both to cook and eat. My mom used to make this for us, and of course she learned how to make it from her mom Nonna Bellino. This is another supremely easy soup to make, that's economic, nourishing, and tasty all at the same time. Enjoy.

PS ... And oh, by-the-way, I myself may love my lentil soup, but I've got to tell you, my dear Uncle Frank, a World War II veteran who served in The United States Marine Corp, and is now, as of this writing 97 years old (Born 1918), Uncle Frank hates Lentils and Lentil Soup. Wanna know why? Of course you do, it's *Uncle Frank.* Well, as I have already stated, my grandparents were poor Italian immigrants from Lercara Friddi, Sicily. They immigrated to America, where Nonno Philipo set up a shoemaker shop on Main Street in Lodi, NJ .. When my mother and her sister Lilly, and brothers Frank, James, and Tony were growing up, I guess you could say, they didn't have much money. So it was soup or pasta for almost every meal, and lentils were served several times a week, every week, in the form of either Lentil Soup or Pasta Lenticchie. As a result of eating lentils, Uncle Frank happens to hate them, that's all there is to it, so, Basta!

RECIPE :

1 pound dry Lentils, washed
1 large Onion, peeled and chopped
¼ cup Olive Oil
2 stalks Celery, washed and chopped
3 Carrots, peeled and cut to 1 " cubes
1 large Potato, peeled and cut to 1" cubes
6 cloves Garlic, peeled and minced
4 quarts water, 2 Chicken Bullion Cubes
6 San Marzano Tomatoes, chopped
1 Bay Leaf
8 Italian Sweet Sausages

Put olive oil, Onions, and Celery in a large 8 quart non-corrosive pot and sauté at low heat for 6 minutes.

Add the Garlic and cook for two minutes more.

Add tomatoes and cook on high heat for 3 minutes.

Add lentils, water, and Bullion Cube if using. Bring up to the boil. Once the liquid is up to the boil, lower heat to medium simmer and cook for 18 minutes.

Meanwhile, cook the sausages in a pan of low simmering water for 10 minutes. Remove and add to pot with the lentils.

Let the lentils continue cooking for another 10 minutes, until they are tender, yet slightly firm and the sausages are cooked through. Turn heat off.

Remove the sausages from the pot and let cool on a plate for a few minutes. Cut sausage into ½" thick pieces and add to the soup.

Ladle the soup into soup bowls, drizzle a little olive oil on top and pass some grated cheese to your guest and yourself.

NOTE: Omit the Sausages and Bullion Cubes from this recipe to make a regular Lentil Soup that is meatless and suitable for vegetarians and during the Lenten Season. You can eat it as is, or add some Escarole for the always-popular Lentil & Escarole Soup. It's oh so good.

Grandma Bellino's Italian Cookbook

ZUPPA di CUCUZZA
"Gagootz" !!!!

This is a soup that my mother used to make every now and then. Usually when her good friend Mary Santangelo gave her a couple big Cucuzza from their backyard garden in Garfield. My mother Lucia learned this recipe from her mother who used to make it back in Sicily, and she learned how to make it from her mother, my Great Grandmother Salemi. This dish is one of the quintessential recipes of this book, and also of both of the Italian-American and Sicilian-American table as a whole, and of course of Sicilians in Sicily as well. The soup is easy to make and quite economical, feeding about 16 portions of which you can serve over 3 to 4 days time. Cucuzza are not always available in every store, however more and more super markets are carrying them during their growing season, and you can always get them at any produce store that specializes in Italian foods.

This dish is a soup of course, but almost a pasta dish as well, and you can vary the amount of pasta as you like. Cooking pasta separately on the side and when you are serving it, you will use double the amount of pasta or more, with less liquid in the soup and using the soup actually as a sauce *to make a pasta dish* if you like. I always do this, as there are always some leftovers when making a pot of it, and serving it as pasta dish is a nice welcome alternative to give one variety from the same dish. I do the same when making Lentil Soup. I make Pasta Lenticchie, which is a pasta dish. In addition, if you like, you can sauté one link of Italian Sweet or Hot Sausage, serve up the soup as either pasta or soup and add a link of sausage or two to each plate. You will love it any way you do, as do the Bellino's & millions of other Italian's have over the years. So make it, enjoy, and always Mangia Bene Amici!

RECIPE :

1 large Cucuzza ak.a. *Gagootz*
1 large onion, peeled and diced
6 Garlic Cloves, peeled and sliced thin
8 tablespoons Olive Oil
½ teaspoon Red Pepper Flakes
1 teaspoon Sea Salt
½ tsp. Black Pepper
6 Plum Tomatoes, chopped
1 pound fresh cooked Fava Beans, or frozen Baby Lima Beans (or canned lima beans)
1 pound imported Italian Ditalini (or Ronzoni)

Cut off ends of the Cucuzza and peel it with a vegetable peeler. Cut the Cucuzza in half lengthwise. Scoop out seeds and discard. Cut the cucuzza in 1 ½ inch cubes.

Put olive oil and the cucuzza in a large 6-quart pot. Cook on medium heat for 5 minutes, occasionally stirring with a wooden spoon. Add onion and cook for 4 minutes more.

Add garlic and cook for 3 minutes. Add red pepper, and cook for 2 minutes.
Add tomatoes and cook on high heat for 5 minutes. Add water and cook on medium-low heat for 12 minutes.

Add Fava Beans (or Lima Beans) and cook on low heat for 6 minutes.

Cook Ditalini according to directions on package. When finished cooking, drain in a colander, making sure to reserve 2 – 3 cups of water to add to soup.

Add all the pasta to the soup. Add salt 7 Black Pepper and stir.

Add water little by little to the soup until you reach the consistency that you like. The soup should be fairly thick, yet slightly watery.

Ladle soup into bowls. Drizzle a bit of olive oil over the top of each bow of soup and pass grated cheese for your guest to put in their soup.

Note : By adding more pasta, varying the amount of water in the soup, and adding if you like sausage to this recipe, you can get several different versions of this dish; as a soup or pasta, with or without meat, all from this one recipe (4 dishes in 1).

ZUPPA di CECI

... *Chickpea Soup*

Soups like this Pasta Ceci, Pasta & Peas, Zuppa di Lenticchie, and Pasta Fagoli were quite popular with early Italian immigrants to the U.S.. Immigrants like my Nonna Giuseppina who immigrated with my Grandfather Philipo in 1904 .. Like most Italian immigrants at the turn of the Century (1900) my grand-parents didn't have much money. They needed to stretch every dollar as far as it would go. They usually couldn't afford meat more than once or twice a week, if that. This Chick Pea Soup, and Lentil Soup, along with Pasta Fazool and the like, provided a means to feed the family a significant meal of sustenance for very little money. These types of soups were the mainstay of the poor for more than 100 years, and are still quite popular today. As I've already stated, my Uncles Tony and Frank didn't care much for lentil soup. I for one, along with my sister Barbara love these soups, especially Zuppa di Lenticchie and this fine Zuppa di Ceci as well. Eat and enjoy.

RECIPE:

1 pound dry Chickpeas, soaked in water overnight
¼ cup Olive Oil
1 medium Onion, peeled and minced fine
6 gloves Garlic, peeled and sliced fine
2 stalks of Celery, washed and minced fine
1 Carrot, peeled and minced
6 San Marzano Tomatoes
1 Bay Leaf
1 teaspoon each of Salt & Black Pepper
5 quarts water
1 pound of Ditalini, or very small Shell Macaroni

Drain beans from water and wash under cold running water for 5 minutes.

Place Olive Oil and Onions in a large 8 quart non-corrosive pot and sauté the onions on medium heat for 5 minutes.

Add Garlic to pot and cook on low heat for 4 minutes.

Add Celery and Carrots and cook on low heat for 7 minutes.

Add tomatoes and cook on high heat for 3 minutes. Add beans, Bay Leaf, and water to the pot and bring up to the boil. Once all comes to the boil, lower heat so the soup is cooking at a low to medium simmer. Cook until the beans are tender, yet slightly firm, about 1 hour 15 minutes to an hour and 30 minutes. After the beans have been cooking for about 55 minutes, cook the pasta according to directions on package. Drain pasta and set aside.

When soup is finished cooking (beans are tender, yet firm), add the cooked pasta to the pot and cook for 6 minutes on low heat.

To serve, fill each persons bowl with soup, and pass Olive Oil to drizzle on top, along with grated Pecorino or Parmigiano Reggiano Cheese.

BONUS DISH : To get two different dishes out of 1, remove 3 ½ cups Chickpeas from pot of soup and drain. Toss with olive oil, vinegar, sliced Red Onion, Cherry Tomatoes, Parsley, Celery, and or Cucumbers, and you've got a nice healthy Insalata di Ceci (Chickpeas Salad).

GRANDMA BELLINO'S CHICKEN SOUP

What's better than chicken soup? Not much I tell you. This is my grandmother's recipe. It's pretty basic, but perfect never-the-less. Make a batch and you're set for good eating, and easy re-heating for the next two or three days. If you want, you can substitute a cup or two of cooked rice for the pasta, or escarole is great instead, which I often do myself. Just wash and chop one head of Escarole, and cook it after you take the chicken out to take the meat off the bones. Or if you don't want to use escarole, and you don't want the noodles, just add more carrots and a couple diced potatoes and you're good to go. This recipe is quite versatile and one everyone needs in their cooking repertoire. It's essential.

RECIPE:

1 whole Chicken
1 medium Onion, peeled and sliced
6 cloves Garlic, peeled
1 Bay Leaf
1 teaspoon Sea Salt
1 tablespoon whole Black Peppercorns
2 stalks Celery, washed and chopped to 1" chunks
5 Carrots, peeled and cut to 1" chunks
3 quarts water
8 ounce package Vermicelli Egg Noodles

Put the chicken in a pot of water with salt and bring to the boil. Lower the heat to a simmer and let simmer 7 minutes. Dump the water and run the chicken under cold water for 5 minutes. This is to clean the chicken.

Drain the chicken and put back into the pot with new fresh water (3 quarts). Add all remaining ingredients, except the pasta. Bring to the boil. Once the water is up to the boil, lower to a simmer and cook the chicken for 1 hours and 15 minutes.

Turn the heat off and let the all sit in the pot for 30 minutes.

Remove chicken from pot and let cool for 12 minutes. Remove all the meat from the chicken. Shred the meat and put back in the pot with the broth and vegetables. Turn heat back on and let simmer at very low heat for 6 minutes.

Cook the pasta according to directions on package. Drain pasta in a colander, and then immediately put the pasta into the pot with the soup.

Serve each person a nice hot bowl of soup. Garnish with a little chopped fresh parsley (optional) if you have it. Save the rest of the soup in containers in the refrigerator to have for breakfast, lunch, or dinner for the next day or two. Will stay in the refrigerator for 5 days or so, and in the freezer for weeks.

TONY'S ESCAROLE & BEAN SOUP
Zuppa di Scarola e Fagioli

This soup is a favorite of most Italian Americans. It's quick and easy to make, hearty, and oh so tasty, and it's Italian-American to the core. You can make it with fresh homemade chicken broth if you have it, or with just water if you're vegetarian, as well as with some canned chicken broth or bullion cubes, it's all good. This is my cousin Anthony Bellino's recipe, it's his favorite soup, and my sister Barbara as well. Make it, and it just might be your favorite soup too.

RECIPE:

4 tablespoons Olive Oil
1 medium Onion, peeled and minced
2 Carrots, peeled and minced fine
4 cloves Garlic, peeled and minced fine
2 cans Lite Chicken Broth
1 quart water, 1 Bay Leaf
½ teaspoon Sea Salt, ½ teaspoon Black Pepper
1 large head Escarole
2 cans Cannellini Beans, drain and wash the beans
¼ cup grated Parmigiano

Place olive oil, onions, and garlic in a 6-quart non-corrosive pot. Turn flame on low and cook for 5 minutes. Add carrots and continue cooking on low heat for 2 minutes.

Add Chicken Broth, water, Bay Leaf, Salt & Black Pepper and turn heat to high. Let boil for 6 minutes.

Cut bottom end off Escarole and discard. Cut the escarole into 1 /12" strips. Wash escarole thoroughly.

Add escarole to pot and cook at a hard boil for 4 minutes.

Add cannellini beans to pot and cook on medium low heat for 8 minutes.

To serve, fill soup bowls with soup. Drizzle a little olive oil over top of soup, and pass around grated Parmigiano Reggiano or Pecorino Romano Cheese.

MACCU
Sicilian Fava Bean Soup

This soup is the pure essence of Sicily. It's cheap and easy to make and is a true peasant dish of Sicily. My grandmother used to make it one or two times a month and get 2 or 3 meals out of it for the whole family as she did with Zuppa di Lenticchie & Pasta e Fagioli. Make a batch of this soup, and you can get several meals as well.

RECIPE:

1 pound dried Fava Beans, cleaned and soak in water overnight
1 medium Onion, peeled and minced fine
¼ cup Olive Oil
3 cloves Garlic, peeled and minced fine
2 Carrots, peeled and chopped fine
2 tablespoons Tomato Paste
1 Bay Leaf.
½ teaspoon Fennel Seeds (optional)
½ to 1 teaspoon each Sea Salt & Black Pepper
Italian Bread, cut in slices and grilled or toasted

Place onions and carrots in a 6-quart non-corrosive pot and cook on low heat for 6 minutes.

Add garlic and cook on low heat for 2 minutes. Remove fava beans from water. Run under cold running water for 4 minutes, and drain again.

Add fava beans to pot, and cover by 2 inches with water. Add tomato paste and Bay Leaf.

Bring to the boil, then lower to a simmer and cook for one hour, stirring occasionally with a wooden spoon, scraping the bottom of pot with the spoon so soup doesn't stick.

Add Fennel Seed and Salt & Black Pepper and continue cooking another 20 minutes until soup is done.

Serve in soup bowls. Top with toasted or grilled Italian Bread that has been rubbed with a garlic clove and has a bit of Olive Oil drizzle on top.

Note: This soup is meant to be a meatless (vegetarian). However, it is perfectly fine to add some meat to it, if you like the soup and want to make a little change. You can dice a 1/4 pound of Pancetta and start the soup with this, sautéing the pancetta before you put in the onions and carrots. Or you can cook a few links of sweet or hot Italian Sausage, and put it into each bowl before you pour the Maccu in. It's all good, any way you serve it.

ZUPPA di BUE e FAGOLI
Beef Pasta & Lima Bean Soup

Pasta, Beans, & Beef in a Soup, what's heartier than that? And tasty too! This is a tasty Sicilian soup that was one of my mother's favorites. Her mother made it for her, and she made it for me, my sister Barbara, and Brothers Jimmy and Michael. Make this tasty soup yourself, and it's sure to become one of your family's favorites too.

RECIPE :

1 large Onion, peeled and diced
1 cup Anellini Pasta (or other tiny pasta shape)
3 Carrots, peeled and cut into large dice
2 Celery Stalks, washed & chopped (optional)
2 Idaho Potatoes, peeled and diced
12 ounce ground Beef Chuck
1 quart Beef Broth
1 ½ quarts water
1 Bay Leaf
½ teaspoon each of Sea Salt & Black Pepper
2 cans Lima Beans, drained and washed
¼ cup Olive Oil
¼ cup fresh Parsley, washed, dried and chopped
¼ cup grated Caciocavallo or Pecorino Cheese

Put olive oil and onions in a 6-quart non-corrosive pot and cook on low heat for 4 minutes.

Add ground beef and cook until rawness of meat disappears, about 7 minutes on low to medium heat.

Add carrots and celery and cook on low heat for 4 minutes.

Add broth, water, potato, and Bay Leaf and cook on low heat for 22 minutes.

Add Lima Beans and cook on low heat for 6 minutes.

Cook the Anelletti according to directions on package. Drained in colander when finished cooking.

Add pasta to soup and mix. Ladle soup into bowls and sprinkle chopped Parsley on top. Pass Olive Oil and grated cheese to sprinkle over soup.

ZUPPA di GIUSEPPINA

This is a nice hearty soup that they make in the town of Lercara Friddi and the surrounding area. The pork provides nice flavor along with the aromatic vegetables and cheese, the beans and pasta make for some good heartiness, as well as stretching the soup out and making it quite affordable. And the beans are one of the healthiest foods you could ever eat. Make a big pot, serve family and friends, and save some for a couple other days of enjoyment later on. It's soup!

RECIPE :

¼ cup Olive Oil
12 ounce ground Pork, or 4 Italian Sweet Sausages
1 medium Onion, peeled and chopped to small dice
4 cloves Garlic, peeled and minced
1/2 pound dry Roman Beans, soak in water 24 hrs.
2 ½ quarts Chicken Broth
2 cups water
1 Bay Leaf
1/2 pound Funghini (small Mushroom Shaped Pasta)
½ teaspoon each of Sea Salt & Black Pepper
¼ cup fresh chopped Italian Parsley

Remove the beans from the water they were soaking in over night, wash under cold running water.
Add olive oil and onion to a 6-quart non-corrosive pot and cook on low heat for 2 minutes.

Add ground pork (or sausage meat) and cook on low heat until the meat is cooked through, about 8 minutes.

Add beans, chicken broth, Bay Leaf, and water to the pot and bring up to the boil.

Lower heat so the soup is cooking at a light low simmer. Let simmer until the beans are cooked (about 55 minutes), being tender yet slightly firm at the same time.

Cook the pasta about 10 minutes and according to directions on package. Drain the pasta in a colander.

Add pasta to the soup and let simmer for 4 minutes.

To serve, ladle soup into bowls, sprinkle on some olive oil and pass grated Pecorino or Parmigiano Reggiano Cheese.

NOTE: If you can't find the Funghini, use any small pasta, like, Ditalini, Conchigliette (tiny shells pasta) Lumanchine (Snails), or Anellini (little rings).

Also if you don't have fresh chicken broth, use half canned or boxed broth and water, or water with chicken bullion cubes.

Daniel Bellino Z

PASTA
We Call It Maccheroni !!!

Pasta? Who doesn't just love it? Just about everyone does. It's the backbone and most loved of all the elements of the wondrous cuisine of Italy. People are enamored with it the World over, be they *Italian* or *not*. If they're not Italian, thus not having the great fortune of having a Nonna and or mother who are great Italian cooks who cook them the wonderful dishes of the Italian cuisines. So, what can one of these poor souls to do (who don't have a relative whose a great Italian cook)? Go to a good Italian Restaurant? There's one big problem there? The cost! Yes, pasta which is oh so cheap, unless making one with shrimp or lobster, most pasta dishes will cost less than $1.00 per portion when made at home. Go to a restaurant and that same pasta will cost 20 times as much, with a plate of pasta on the lower end, with an average of $16.00, and on the high-end about $24 to $26, and that doesn't include the tax and tip. So, if you're eating in a restaurant, a plate of pasta like Spaghetti Bolognese that would only cost about one dollar a plate at home, will end up costing maybe $29 or so, once you add the cost of the pasta on the menu, the tax, and tip, of that same pasta that would cost just a Dollar a plate at home, it can end up costing you 30 times that in a restaurant. Now multiply that by a family of four and we're talking $120 or more for what you can make for just $10. Wow! That's why many of us Italian, do not often eat pasta in Italian restaurants unless we're having some sort of family get-together. We just can not see *paying so much,* for something that cost so little, and something that we probably make better at home. If you're like me, when you do eat out, it's most often at some Asian Restaurant; like Chinese, Vietnamese, Thai, or Indian. Hey it's great to eat out, but we eat a lot of pasta, almost everyday (in years past), so we'd have to be rich to eat pasta out in a restaurant as often as we must have our bowl. And like I said, that's almost every day. Well, it used to be anyway. I know, I wanted it, craved it, and ate pasta almost everyday for years. Well now, with the way things are nowadays, and we know that too much flour isn't the best thing for you, we have like many others cut down on our consumption. Cut down, but not eliminated. "I'm not about to start eating gluten-free pasta. No way!" Instead of eating *pasta* 5 or 6 times a week like I used, I've almost cut that in half. Before, where I used to eat pasta about six times a week, and not just one serving, I'd often have a 2nd helpings, and even thirds for a total of, I'd estimate about 11-12 servings of Pasta (Maccheroni) a week. My cousin Joe would have even more. These days I eat pasta about 3 and sometimes four times a week. I usually will eat 1 full or ¾ of a serving when I do, and never have 1 ½ to 2 ½ portion sizes as I did in the past. It doesn't mean that I don't still love my maccheroni, *I do, b*ut these days I have to cut down. Pasta and all maccheroni are a huge part of my life, I was practically weaned on it, when my mother served me little Pastina when I was just a tiny little toddler. I've loved it my entire childhood and still do to this very day I'll have a bowl of Pastina, all covered with Butter & Parmigiano of course. Yumm!!!

When it came to the Bellino Family meals, I'm talking about when my mother, her sister Lilly, and her brothers Frank, Tony, and Jimmy and when they were growing up, Nonna Giuseppina cooked all her Sicilian and Italian Soups, and plates of Maccheroni more than anything. For lunch and almost every night at that, it was soup or pasta, the cheapest meal one could put on the table. Pasta is not only delicious; it sustains and was the main-staple of Italians in Italy and in America for many years. And everyone loves pasta, not just Italians. There are many favorites, like: Lasagna, Spaghetti with Meatballs or with Tomato Sauce, Linguine Vongole, Cavatelli, Raviolis, Orecchiette w/Sausage & Broccoli Rabe, Gnocchi, Carbonara, Amatriciana, and on-and-on, "Who doesn't Love Pasta?" "No one I tell you!"

So here you go my friends, my Nonna Giuseppina Bellino's fabulous Pasta Recipes. You're gonna just love them!

SALSA di POMODORO alla NONNA
Grandma's Tomato Sauce

Salsa di Pomodoro, or Tomato Sauce as most people know it, along with pasta are the undisputed backbones of Italian Cuisine and of Italian-American Cuisine in particular, which is based on the cuisine of the motherland *Italy*. But there are differences and variations between the two. You will find this basic tomato sauce called for in many dishes, like; Eggplant Parmigiano, in some types of Lasagna, and baked Maccheroni, in dishes like both; Chicken or Veal Parmigiano, and many more to boot.

There are a number of different versions of Tomato Sauce known as either Salsa Pomodoro or Sugo di Pomodoro in Italy, and as Tomato Sauce, or simply *Sauce* in the Italian-American community. This recipe is for Tomato Sauce in its simplest form, using Olive Oil that's flavored with a little Garlic and Pepperoncino (Red Pepper Flakes) to season the oil, which seasons the tomatoes along with Basil (Basilico), or as the Neapolitans say, *"Baz-see-ne-kole!"*

Many Italian-Americans and most Americans not of Italian ancestry like and think that Oregano is a standard and a *must-have* ingredient in Tomato Sauce, *it is not,* but if you like it, go right ahead and put it in. In Italy, you rarely see Oregano in Sugo di Pomodoro, and this is how the recipe is here.

RECIPE:

3 - 28 oz. cans San Marzano crushed tomatoes
or other good quality Italian style tomatoes
6 cloves minced garlic
1 small onion, minced
½ teaspoon crushed red pepper
¼ cup virgin olive oil
¼ cup chopped fresh basil or 1 teaspoon dried
Sea Salt and Black Pepper to taste

In a 6 quart or larger pot, sauté onions over a low flame for 3 minutes. Add garlic and cook for 3-4 minutes. Do not let the garlic get dark or burn. Add red pepper flakes and cook 1 minute.

Add tomatoes, turn heat up to high and stir. When sauce starts to bubble, turn flame down so the sauce is at a low simmer. Simmer for 35 minutes while frequently stirring the bottom of the pan to keep sauce from burning. Add fresh basil in the last ten minutes of cooking.

Cook whatever pasta you choose (spaghetti is best) according to directions on package. Drain pasta, toss with tomato sauce and a drizzle of olive oil, plate, and serve with cheese.

SPAGHETTI w/ TOMATO SAUCE & *HOW to COOK PASTA*

Spaghetti with Tomato Sauce is most likely without much questioning at all, thee single most popular of the many loved and often eaten dishes of Italian Cuisine, and this includes not just Italian-Americans but just about all Americans, some 300 Million or so, everybody loves Italian Food. And there are no dishes more popular than Pizza and the ever-present Spaghetti with Tomato Sauce. This being said, there are many travesties committed every single day in the name of Tomato Sauce, Spaghetti Pomodoro (Spaghetti w/Tomatoes) and Italian Cuisine. What many American's might think is a good plate of pasta, most Italian-Americans would feel is awful, sacrilegious, and *not authentic*.

Believe it or not, there is quite an art to making a good, and even perfect plate of Spaghetti. I know for a fact that many Americans are afraid of cooking pasta and can't get a handle on it. Well it's not that hard, but there is *a right way* and a *wrong way,* and pasta must be done right to be good, and to be perfect, or as close to perfect as possible. It must be right.

Following are a few simple rules to get you on your way. Number 1, you always should have a good amount of water to cook the pasta in. You need 3 & a half to 4 quarts of water to cook one pound of pasta in and the water should be heavily salted. Number two, never put pasta into water that is not at a heavy rolling boil. Continue cooking the pasta at a heavy rolling boil the whole time you are cooking it, and stir occasionally with a wood spoon. Do not add olive oil to the water, just salt. Look at the package and cook according to the directions on the pasta package. Start tasting and testing the doneness of the pasta about two minutes before it says the cooking time is on the package. The way you do this is by taking a piece of the pasta (spaghetti, rigatoni, etc.) from the water, quickly cool it under running water and then biting into it to see where it is in its cooking stage, and if it needs a minute or two more to cook. Bite into another piece in another 60 or 90 seconds, and if the pasta is done and ready, turn off the heat, drain the pasta into a colander, shake the colander, put the pasta back into the pot it cooked in, add a tablespoon or so of olive oil and stir the pasta, add some of the sauce, then evenly divide the pasta among 4-6 plates for your guest. Top each plate (bowl) of pasta with some more of the sauce, give each person their pasta, and pass around some grated cheese, if the pasta requires it (never any cheese for Pasta with Clam Sauce or any Seafood Pasta). Please?

NOTE: These directions are for dry package pasta. For fresh pasta such as; Ravioli, Tagliarini, Fettuccine, and such, the cooking time is shorter as the pasta is not dried and hard. Fresh pasta is much softer than dried pasta (Pasta Asciutta). For example, fettuccine in most instances will take about 4-5 minutes to cook, as opposed to about double that for spaghetti and other dry pasta that takes about 10 – 12 minutes to cook. Also note, that *only dry pasta can be cooked al dente* and fresh pasta cannot be made al dente as it never gets hard and thus can not be hard (al dente "To the Bite") in the center as dry pasta such as spaghetti can.

Now go at it. Cook some, don't be afraid, follow my instructions, and good luck. Basta la Pasta!

SPAGHETTI POMODORO
Spaghetti w/ Tomato Sauce

RECIPE :

1 pound Imported Italian Spaghetti
4 quarts water (for cooking the Spaghetti)
3 cups Tomato Sauce, recipe page
Grated Parmigiano Reggiano or Pecorino Romano
Olive Oil & Salt

To make a great plate of Spaghetti Pomodoro follow these directions.

Bring a large pot of salted water to the boil. Heat the Tomato Sauce in a separate pot or pan.

Put the Spaghetti into the pot with rapidly boiling water and cook according to directions on package. Start testing the doneness of the spaghetti 1 ½ to 2 minutes before the cooking time on package. You do this by pulling a strand of spaghetti out of the pot and biting into it to test the doneness.

When the spaghetti is done, drain it into a colander, reserving a bit of the pasta cooking water.

Put pasta back in pot it cooked in. Add a few drops of olive oil and mix. Add half the tomato sauce and mix. Plate the Spaghetti equally amongst four plates. Top each plate with an equal portion of remaining sauce. Pass the grated cheese and enjoy a perfect plate of Spaghetti Pomodoro.

SPAGHETTI & MEATBALLS

What can be said about Spaghetti & Meatballs that has not already been? Actually, quite a bit I guess. Millions of Italian Americans probably have a story or two, and an opinion on the subject. Spaghetti & Meatballs is near the top of the food-chain when it comes to Italian-American Food and the dishes that we love most. For some, this dish is tops. When it comes to we Sicilian-Americans, *Meatballs* are of utmost importance and a dish we love as much or more than any other. When Meatballs are at the top of their game, made by Italian ladies like my Nonna Giuseppina, my Aunt Helen, or Aunt Fran, there are not many things in this whole wide world that one could love more. And we do *love our Meatballs,* and just the way momma makes them. Meatballs can be eaten on their own, as a Hot Antipasto, as Italians in Italy seem to do more often than we Italians in America do. We love them with Spaghetti in the iconic dish *Spaghetti & Meatballs*, in the Sunday Sauce, a.k.a. *Gravy*, or on a sandwich in the form of our beloved *Meatball Parm*. You can even have them as a main-course with mashed potatoes. Yes we love them in the Sunday Sauce, in Sandwiches, and antipasto too. Hey, they're Meatballs, what's not to love?

MEATBALLS

The RECIPE :

1 lb. ground Beef
½ lb. ground Veal, ½ lb. Ground Pork
4 Tbs. fresh Italian Parsley, chopped
1 minced onion, 2 cloves garlic, minced
4 Tablespoons plain breadcrumbs
2 large eggs, ¼ cup Milk
Salt & Pepper, ½ cup grated Parmigiano

In a small bowl, break and beat eggs. Add breadcrumbs and milk and let soak for 10 minutes.

In a large bowl, add all the remaining ingredients. Add eggs and mix well with your hands.

Shape meat mixture to from balls that are about 3 inches in diameter.

Coat the bottom of a cookie sheet or roasting pan with a thin film of olive oil. Cook Meatballs at 350 degrees for 10 minutes.

Take meatballs out of oven and simmer on low heat for 45 minutes in a batch of Tomato Sauce or Sunday Sauce (Gravy).

NOTE: This is a base recipe. If you like you can alter it, as you can for most recipes. If you like, you can use only ground beef only and not use veal or pork at all. If you want, you can make them with just beef and pork, even just veal, which is the preferred way in Tuscany. If you don't like garlic omit it. This recipe above is how my Nonna made her Meatballs, it's the way my Mother Lucia did, and it's the way I do, but to each his own.

SPAGHETTI w/ GARLIC & ANCHOVIES
Al Pacino's Favorite Pasta !!!

This simple pasta is without question along with its sister dish of Spaghetti w/ Garlic & Oil one of Italian-America's most preferred dishes. We just love it! We love it most of all for its wonderful taste, but also for *its quick and easy preparation* and for the fact that we can have it anytime we like, as we always have all the ingredients needed to make it stored in our dry-goods cabinet. This is two recipes in one, the Spaghetti with Garlic Oil & Anchovies is one, and by omitting the anchovies in this recipe, you can make Spaghetti Aglio Olio which is actually the more popular of the two, and Al's favorite.

If you make this dish of Spaghetti w/Garlic Oil & Anchovies and add toasted breadcrumbs sprinkled over the top, then you'll have one of the favorite dishes of Saint Joseph's Day, which falls on March 19th each year.

My mother Lucia loved this dish quite a bit and made it often, as it was taught to her by her mom. And for those of you who may not know, Spaghetti Aglio e Olio is a popular dish that Italians in Italy, especially in Rome love to cook late night after they get home from *a night on the town,* and they have a case of the munchies. You can do the same as well.

RECIPE:

¼ cup best quality Italian Olive Oil
6 cloves of Garlic, peeled and minced
½ teaspoon Red Pepper Flakes
6 Anchovy Filets minced fine
1 pound imported Italian Spaghetti
¼ cup Italian Parsley

Put a large pot with 4 quarts of water on the stove. Add 2 tablespoons salt and bring to the boil.

Place Olive Oil and Anchovies in a large frying pan and cook on medium heat for 2 minutes.

Add garlic and cook on medium heat for 2 minutes. Add red pepper and continue cooking on low heat until the garlic begins to turn slightly brown. Turn heat off and let rest.

Add spaghetti to the boiling salted water. Cook spaghetti according to directions on package. Two minutes before the cooking time on package start testing the doneness of the spaghetti by taking a strand out of the water and biting into it to see how far cooked it. By doing this you'll be able to determine if it needs to cook a bit longer or if it's ready.

Once the past is finished cooking, quickly remove it from the heat and drain into a colander, reserving about 4 tablespoons of the pasta cooking water to add to pasta sauce.

Add spaghetti back to the pot it cooked in and drizzle on a little olive oil and mix. Pour the garlic anchovy sauce and the reserved pasta water over the spaghetti with half the chopped Parsley and mix well.

Divide the spaghetti among four pasta plates or bowls. Sprinkle the top of each plate of Spaghetti with some chopped parsley and serve.

AL PACINO & AGLIO OLIO

Al Pacino and Aglio Olio you ask? What about it? Well it's just that Spaghetti Aglio Olio always reminds me of that great fellow New Yorker Sicilian American, the one-and-only Al Pacino from da Bronx. It's not a big deal, just a wonderful little memory for me. When I was the Wine Director at the famed *Barbetta Restorante* on Restaurant Row in New York's Theater District (where Al often performs on stage), Al Pacino used to come and eat there every now and then. He never wanted anything to fancy, but something that just about all true blooded Italian-American wants, and that dish is Spaghetti Aglio Olio, plain and simple, yet it's *in our blood*. That's what *Al* wanted and that's what we gave him, and Al loved it and you will too.

Note: As has already been noted, you can make Spaghetti w/ Garlic & Oil, simply by making the above recipe, and omitting the Anchovies, and you'll have it just like Al Pacino does. Enjoy!

PASTA alla NORMA

After the Cannoli, Pasta con Sarde, and Caponata are Sicily's most popular dishes. Pasta alla Norma comes in 4th on the list, making it quite popular as well. This is my grandmother's recipe. This dish was named for Vincenzo Bellini's opera Norma. My grandmother cooked many meals that came from the vegetables of my grandfather's garden. The vegetable garden provided both the freshest and most economical ingredients that any Italian-American with limited funds could ever wish to have, while being the healthiest as well. Everything in this dish was from the garden except for the dry pasta and the cheese. The recipe shows San Marzano as an ingredient, but my grandma Giuseppina used tomatoes from their jarred tomato passata made from the garden grown tomatoes, that were canned in late August and September. You can do the same if you have some garden tomatoes, otherwise use the canned San Marzano Tomatoes from the groeria, and enjoy this favored Sicilian pasta.

RECIPE :

2 medium Eggplants, washed and cut into ¾" cubes
1 small Onion, peeled and diced
5 cloves Garlic, peeled and sliced thin
½ teaspoon Red Pepper Flakes
1 – 28 can San Marzano Tomatoes
8 tablespoons Olive Oil, Salt & Black Pepper
12 fresh Basil Leaves, washed and torn
1 pound Italian Bucatini (or other pasta)

Turn oven on to 450 degrees. Place eggplant on a cookie sheet with a third of the olive oil and mix to coat the eggplant. Cook eggplant for 15 minutes at 450 degrees.

Sprinkle eggplant with a little more olive oil and stir. Cook eggplant another 8 minutes.

Remove eggplant from oven and set on counter to cool. Season the eggplant with a little Sea Salt and Black Pepper to taste. Mix eggplant and set aside.

Place remaining olive oil in a 6-quart pot with the chopped onions and cook on low heat for 6 minutes.

Add garlic and cook on low heat for 2 minutes. Add red pepper flakes and cook on very low heat for 1 minute.

Add tomatoes to pot and turn heat to high. Cook on high heat while stirring with a wooden spoon for 5 minutes. Lower the heat to a low flame and cook tomatoes for 15 minutes.

Add eggplant and Basil to pot with tomatoes and cook on a low flame for 6 minutes.

Cook Bucatini or other pasta, according to direction on package. When the pasta is done cooking, drain in a colander, and shake off excess water.

Add the drain pasta back to the pot it cooked in, sprinkle with a little olive oil and stir.

Add half the sauce to the pasta and mix. Plate pasta in equal portions onto 4 plates. Add a little more sauce to top the pasta. Grate the Ricotta Salata over each portion of pasta, using the large holes of a box grater.

Grandma Bellino's Italian Cookbook

PASTA con CUCUZZA
Pasta with Gagootz !!!

Pasta & Gagootz is a long time favorite with the Bellino Family. Cucuzza, a.k.a. *Gagootz* is oh so Sicilian, and third only to Eggplant (Melanzane) and Artichokes, as the most popular and loved vegetable of all. Well yes there's tomatoes and we love cauliflower quite a bit too, but Gagootz? Yes Cucuzza is the big Italian Squash eaten mainly by Italian-Americans, and mostly those only of Sicilian and Neapolitan origins. Even in the Italian-American community, still not many people know of this amazing Baseball Bat sized vegetable that Sicilians like to eat. So yes Cucuzza is ours, we Sicilians and other Southern Italian peoples, but not everyone you see. Hey, we love to share, but once in a while we like to keep a few things to ourselves. Doesn't everyone? My mom used to make this often, along with Zuppa di Cucuzza from her mothers traditional recipes from Lercara Friddi. The recipe is oh so Sicilian, tasty and whimsical too. If you make it, you and your guest are sure to love it, as we Bellino's have for more than 100 years now. Mangia Bene!

RECIPE : PASTA GAGOOTZ

1 large Cucuzza (Italian Squash)
1 medium Onion, peeled and chopped
¼ cup Olive Oil
1 teaspoon Red Pepper Flakes
4 cloves Garlic, peeled and sliced
1 – 28 ounce can crushed tomatoes
1 pound Green Beans, cleaned and cut in half
¼ cup fresh Basil leaves torn in half
1/3 cup grated Pecorino Romano Cheese

Peel the Cucuzza with a vegetable peeler and scoop out large seeds if there are any and discard. Cut the Cucuzza (Gagootz) into 1 ½" pieces.

Place Cuccuzza and olive oil in a 6-quart pot and cook on low heat for 5 minutes. Add onion and cook for 4 minutes more.

Add garlic and cook on low flame for 2 minutes. Add red pepper flakes and cook 1 minute while stirring.

Add tomatoes and cook for 20 minutes, stirring occasionally with a wooden spoon.

While the sauce is simmering cook the green beans in a large pot of boiling salted water for 3 minutes. Drain the beans in a colander and put in the pot of sauce after it has been simmering for 12 minutes. Continue cooking for a total cooking time of 35-40 minutes for the sauce.

Add basil and cook two minutes.

Cook pasta according to directions on package. When finished cooking, drain the pasta in a colander, reserving about 7 tablespoons of the pasta cooking water.

Put the pasta back in the pot it cooked in. Drizzle on a little olive oil and mix. Add 1/3 of the sauce to the pot with the pasta and mix.

Divide the pasta among four plates. Top each plate of pasta with a little more of the sauce. Give a plate to each guest, pass the grated cheese and enjoy.

PASTA LENTICCHIE
Pasta with Lentils

Pasta Lenticchie is a standby of many Italian American families, just as it's sister soup, Zuppa di Lenticchie (Lentil Soup). As is with many of the older Italian-American recipes that are primarily from the south, including from; Sicily, Campania (around Naples), Apulia, and Calabria, this is a dish of the poor (Cucina Povera), as all the ingredients, other than the cheese are quite cheap. And for those families who couldn't afford cheese, they simply didn't use it. They might use toasted breadcrumbs instead, from some leftover bread. Nowadays just about anyone can afford cheese, so we highly recommend you dressing your pasta with a drizzle of Olive Oil and some grated Pecorino or Caciocavallo Cheese, it's oh so tasty.

RECIPE :

8 ounce dry Lentils
8 tablespoons Olive Oil
1 medium Onion, peeled and minced fine
2 stalks Celery, washed and minced fine
5 cloves Garlic, peeled and minced fine
1 cup chopped San Marzano Plum Tomatoes
2 Chicken Bullion Cubes (optional)
1 Bay Leaf
1 – 10 ounce package frozen Spinach, thawed
1 pound Pasta; Gemelli, Small Shells, or Fusilli
grated Pecorino Romano, Parmigiano, or Grana

Place ¼ cup of olive oil and onions in a large 6 quart pot. Cook on low heat for 5 minutes, stirring occasionally.

Add Celery and cook for 4 minutes. Add red pepper cook and garlic and cook for 2 minutes.

Add tomatoes and cook on high heat for 4 minutes. Add Lentils and cook 3 minutes while stirring with a wooden spoon.

Add Bay Leaf and water to cover the lentils by 1 inch. Cook at a medium simmer until lentils are tender but have a bit of firmness to them, about 22 minutes.

Chop the thawed spinach, add to lentils and cook for 5 minutes on medium heat.

Cook pasta as per the directions on package. When finished cooking, drain into a colander, reserving a few tablespoons of water to add to pasta.

Put the drained pasta back into the pot it cook in and drizzle with some Olive Oil. Using a large slotted spoon, add lentils to the past and mix. Add a little bit of the pasta cooking water if you need it. You don't want the pasta to be watery, but you do want it to be a little loose. Do this by adding only small amounts of liquid at a time until you have reached the consistency that you like.

Plate into shallow past bowls, drizzle with a bit more olive oil and pass the grated cheese.

NOTE: This is a vegetarian dish, but if you like to add meat, you can sauté some Italian Sausages and add to this recipe. Add some sausage to each bowl and enjoy.

PASTA con SALSICCIA e MELANZANE
Cavatappi w/ Sausage & Eggplant

RECIPE :

2 medium Eggplants, washed and cut to 1 inch cubes with the skin on (do not peel)
1/2 cup Olive Oil
6 Sweet Italian Sausages, removed from casing
4 cloves of Garlic, peeled and left whole
½ teaspoon Red Pepper flakes
1 – 28 oz. can San Marzano Tomatoes
12 fresh Basil leaves
1 pound imported Italian Cavatappi (or other pasta)
grated Pecorino Romano or Granna Padano cheese

Put half the Olive Oil in a large frying pan and cook the eggplant in two separate batches. Cook the eggplant at high heat, stirring occasionally but not too often in order to let the eggplant brown. Set aside when done.

Place remaining olive oil in a 6-quart pot with the garlic. Break the sausage into pieces and put in pot. Cook on medium heat until the sausage meat is cooked through.

Add Red Pepper and cook one minute. Drain the tomatoes from the watery juice in can, reserving the liquid until later. Chop tomatoes to medium size chunks.

Add tomatoes to pot and cook on high heat for 5 minutes, stirring constantly. Add eggplant, reserve tomato liquid, lower heat to low and let simmer for 16 minutes on low heat.

Turn heat off and add fresh basil that you have torn in half each leaf. Stir to mix.

Cook Rigatoni according to directions on package. When finished cooking, drain rigatoni (pasta) in a colander, reserve a few tablespoons of pasta water.

Put the rigatoni back in the pot it cooked in. Drizzle a bit of olive oil of the rigatoni and mix. Add half the sauce to the pasta and mix.

Divide the Rigatoni among 4 to 6 plates, depending on the size portion you'd like to serve. Add a bit more sauce on top of the pasta and serve, passing grating cheese of choice.

SPAGHETTI with BROCCOLI

This is a dish similar to a Southern Italian favorite Orecchiette w/ Broccoli Rabe & Sausage. This dish is made with regular Broccoli rather than the bitter Rapini (Broccoli Rabe). It is fast and easy to make. On top of that it's really tasty and quite healthy too. I once made it for my friend Jimmy and his girlfriend. Jimmy loved it so much, I taught him how to make it, and he makes it at least once every week, sometimes twice. It's just that the dish is tasty, inexpensive, healthy, quick and easy to make.

RECIPE :

2 heads fresh Broccoli. 6 cloves thinly sliced garlic
¼ cup olive oil, ¼ teaspoon crushed red pepper
1 ½ lbs. good quality imported Italian Spaghetti
¼ cup grated Parmigiano Reggiano
1/3 stick of butter

Wash broccoli and cut into florets. Blanch Broccoli in boiling salted for 3 minutes.

Drain broccoli in a strainer. Place olive oil and garlic in a large frying pan. Sauté over low heat until the garlic just start browning. Add broccoli and sauté over medium heat for about 6 minutes.

While the broccoli is sautéing, cook spaghetti in a large pot of water according to directions on the package.

Drain spaghetti and add to pan with Broccoli. Add butter and toss. Plate Spaghetti with Broccoli and pass around the Grated Cheese.

NOTE: A variation on this dish is to add 1 cup of cooked Tomato Sauce to the spaghetti after draining it from the water. Plate the Spaghetti into six plates or pasta bowls, divide the sautéed broccoli evenly on top of each portion of Spaghetti and serve.

SPAGHETTI PICCHI PACCHIU

This is a lovely way to make pasta with tomatoes that is super quick and easy and features fresh ripe Cherry Tomatoes. This particular kind of tomato sauce is the *freshest tomato sauce of all*. This is a big favorite of Sicilians especially during the hot months of Summer.

1 pint ripe Cherry Tomatoes, washed and cut in half
1/3 cup Olive Oil
5 Garlic Cloves, peeled an sliced thin
½ teaspoon of Pepperoncino (Red Pepper flakes)
½ teaspoon Sicilian Sea Salt
¼ cup fresh torn Basil Leaves
1 pound imported Italian Spaghetti

Place the garlic and olive oil in a pan and cook on low heat for 3 minutes. Add Red Pepper Flakes and Tomatoes and cook on high heat for 6-7 minutes while stirring with a wooden spoon. Add Basil and cook on low heat 1 minute. Turn heat off and let set.

Cook the spaghetti in boiling salted water according to directions on package. When done, drain, reserving about 5 tablespoons of the pasta cooking water.

Add the drained spaghetti and reserved pasta water to pan with tomatoes and olive oil and mix.

Plate spaghetti onto 4 plates and serve. Eat as is, or sprinkle a little Pecorino Romano Cheese on top.

VARIATION : This pasta is great with some fresh mozzarella, of which is the way they like to serve it on the beautiful island of Capri as well as in Sorrento and in and around Naples and the Amalfi Coast.

To serve the spaghetti this way which you may know as Spaghetti alla Caprese, cut ½ pound of fresh Mozzarella into small cubes. When you add the spaghetti to the pan with the tomatoes, add the mozzarella as well and toss to mix. Serve on 4 to 6 plates, and garnish with a Basil Flower on top of each plate if you have some.

Enjoy the Spaghetti with a nice bottle of Southern Italian White Wine and pretend you're in Sicily, Napoli, or Capri. What's better than that?

Suggested Wines : Falanghina or Greco di Tufo.

PASTA con PATATE
Pasta & Potatoes

Pasta & Potatoes is an old Sicilian *peasant dish* (la Cucina Povera) that they eat all over the south of Italy, making slightly different variations depending on the region. Some add carrots & celery in the preparation, some use more tomato, and some don't use tomato at all. This one uses a little bit of tomato in this Sicilian recipe from Polizzi Generosa. My mother said that my grandmother made it all the time, which I'm sure she did, as they didn't have much money and this was one of the cheapest dishes of all. Cheap, but tasty and soul satisfying. Try it!

RECIPE :

4 large Baking Potatoes
1 large Onion, peeled and chopped
¼ cup Olive Oil
¼ teaspoon Pepperoncino
12 ounces Ditalini Pasta
3 whole San Marzano Tomatoes, chopped
Salt & Black Pepper to taste
¾ cup grated Pecorino Romano

Peel potatoes and cut into ¼" cubes. Place in a pot of boiling salted water and cook for 2 minutes at the boil. Drain in colander and shake off excess water.

Place olive oil in a 6-quart pot with the onions and cook on low heat for 7 minutes. Add potatoes to pot and cook on high heat for 4 minutes while stirring. Add chopped tomatoes and cook on high heat for 4 minutes.

Add water so it comes about ½" over the potatoes. Bring all to the boil. Cook potatoes at a steady simmer for 15 minutes, at which time there should be just a little liquid in the pot and the potatoes are cooked and a creamy liquid has formed. If too dry, add a bit more water.

You should be cooking the Ditalini in rapidly boiling salted water as the potatoes are cooking. Cook the ditalini to 1 minute less then the directions on package call for. Turn heat off and drain pasta in a colander, reserve a 1/2 a cup of pasta cooking water.

Add ditalini to potatoes, add a few tablespoons of olive oil and cook on medium heat for two minutes while stirring. Turn heat off. Add half the cheese, and mix.

Plate Pasta & Potatoes on to each persons plate. Drizzle a little olive oil over the top of the pasta and pass around some grated Pecorino.

VARIATION : If you'd like, you can add ¼ to ½ pound cooked Pancetta to this recipe, or cook about 6 Sausage Links that have been remove from casings, crumbled-up, cooked and added to the potatoes when the pasta is put in, it's tasty any way you choose.

PASTA con CAVOLO e SALSICCIA
Ziti with Cabbage & Sausage

RECIPE:

½ head of Savoy Cabbage, cored and shredded
¼ cup Olive Oil, Salt & Pepper
5 cloves Garlic, peeled and sliced
1 pound Sweet Italian Sausage, skin removed
2 cups Tomato Sauce, ½ cup grated Pecorino Cheese
1 pound Ziti or other pasta

Cook Cabbage in boiling salted water for 6 minutes.

Remove sausages from casing and cook in a pan with a little olive oil on medium heat, breaking up the sausage. Cook until sausage loses raw color, about 8 minutes, season with Salt & Pepper. Set aside.

Place the remaining olive oil in pan with garlic and cook on low heat for three minutes. Add drained cabbage and cook on medium heat for 6 minutes. Season with Salt & Pepper. Add tomato sauce & Sausage to pan and cook on low heat for 8 minutes.

As the sauce is cooking, cook the pasta according to directions on package. Drain pasta when finished.

Add pasta back to the pot it cooked in. Add half the sauce to the pot and mix with pasta.

To serve, plate pasta with sauce onto 4-6 plates. Top with a bit more sauce, and pass around grated cheese.

MACCHERONI con CAVOLFIORE

PASTA with CAULIFLOWER

You don't see this dish all that much in any Italian restaurants in America, or homes other than in Sicily and some but not all Sicilian-American households. In the Bellino and Cavallo families, there always was.

Recipe:

1 large head cauliflower, core and cut into 1-1/2" pieces
10 cloves of garlic, peeled
1-28 oz. can crushed San Marzano Tomatoes
1 medium onion, minced
½ teaspoon crushed red pepper flakes
¼ cup olive oil, salt and pepper to taste

OPTIONAL BREADCRUMB TOPPING

6 tablespoons Olive Oil
2 cloves Garlic, peeled and minced fine
½ plain Breadcrumbs

Place half the oil in a large pot with the minced onions. Sauté for three minutes. Add five cloves of garlic that have been thinly sliced. Sauté for 3 minutes over low heat. Add Red Pepper, sauté for 2 minutes.

Add tomatoes and simmer over low heat for 25 minutes.

While tomato sauce is simmering, place remainder of olive oil in a large frying pan and sauté the cauliflower over medium heat for 12-15 minutes until it is slightly browned.

Add remaining Five whole Garlic cloves with the Cauliflower, and sauté for about 5 minutes. Add salt and pepper to taste.

Add cauliflower to tomato sauce and cook for 10 minutes.

You can use almost any pasta for this sauce, but short pasta is best, such as Rigatoni, Orecchietti, Ditalini, and or Cavatappi work best.

Cook the pasta according to directions on package. Drain the pasta in a colander. Put pasta back in the pot it cooked in, then add ¾ of the sauce over pasta and mix.

To serve, plate the pasta, topping each plate with some additional Cauliflower Sauce. Pass the grated Pecorino Romano or Parmigiano Reggiano Cheese.

Note: The Breadcrumb topping is optional if you'd like to use it. The breadcrumb topping is quite tradition in Sicilian Pasta dishes as it came about as a substitute for grated cheese, which was too expensive for many Sicilians in years past, so they used these breadcrumbs. Try it sometimes, it's makes for a nice alternative.

PASTA con PESTO TRAPANESE
Pasta with Trapani Style Pesto

4 ounce blanched Almonds
¼ each teaspoon Sea Salt & Black Pepper
2 cloves Garlic, peeled
1 cup fresh Basil, washed and dried
8 ounces Cherry Tomatoes
4-5 tablespoon Olive Oil
1 pound Spaghetti or short pasta of your choice

Add Almonds and Garlic to a Food Processor and pulse until almonds are very finely chopped.

Add Basil and Salt and pulse until very fine.

Add Tomatoes and Olive Oil and pulse until all the contents is in a fine paste. Taste to see if you need to season further with Salt & Black Pepper.

Cook pasta according to directions on package. When finished cooking drain pasta in a colander, reserving a bit of water to add to pasta & pesto.

Return pasta back to the pot it cooked in. Add ¾ of the pesto and mix. Add a bit of the water if you need it and mix. Serve onto 4-6 plates depending on the portion size you'd like to serve. Top each plate of pasta with a bit more pesto and serve. "You're in Sicily!"

PASTA CUI VROCCOLI ARRIMINATI
Sicilian Pasta w/ Cauliflower

Here's another wonderful Sicilian Pasta dish made with Cauliflower. It's a bit different from the previous Cauliflower Pasta recipe. Cauliflower is the starring main-ingredients, but the flavorings of the dish are quite different, whereas the first recipe is with tomato, this one has no tomato and is flavored by the very Sicilian ingredients of; Anchovies, Currants, Pignoli, and Saffron. You gotta try this one, and make it for your friends who might like to taste something very different from the norm.

INGREDIENTS :

1 head Cauliflower, ¼ cup Olive Oil
7 cloves Garlic, peeled and left whole
4 – 6 Anchovy Filets, minced fine
1/3 cup chopped fresh Italian Parsley
2 tablespoons Pignoli Nuts
4 tablespoons Golden Currants, soaked in warm water for 15 minutes
Toasted Breadcrumbs (optional)
1 pound Cavatappi, Buccatini or other Pasta

Remove the root from the Cauliflower and cut into 1" pieces. Put in a large bowl with 1/4 cup olive oil and 4 garlic cloves, and mix. Put on to a large cookie sheet and roast in the oven at 375 degrees for 20 minutes until the cauliflower is golden brown and is slightly tender when pierced with a fork, yet slightly firm.

Add remaining olive oil, garlic, and the Anchovies, to a large frying pan and cook on medium heat for 3 minutes. Add red pepper and cook on low heat for 1 minute. Add Pignoli Nuts, Saffron, and drained Currants to pan and cook for 3 minutes.

Cook the pasta following the directions on box. When finished cooking, drain and reserve 4 tablespoons of pasta cooking water.

Put the pasta and the reserved water back in the pot the pasta cooked in. Add all the sauce and the Parsley to the pasta and mix.

Plate the pasta on 4-6 plates and serve. If using toasted breadcrumbs, put on table and let each person sprinkle them on if they'd like to. Do not serve this pasta with cheese.

NOTE : *Vroccoli* is not the Italian but the Sicilian dialect word for *Cauliflower.*

NOTE II : Bucatini is the most traditional pasta for this dish, but many (including me) prefer eating it with short maccheroni, and my favorite for this dish is Cavatappi. Use whatever you like best, and enjoy.

SPAGHETTI with ZUCCHINI

RECIPE :

1 large Onion, peeled and chopped
¼ cup Olive Oil
3 medium Zucchini, washed, cut in 1 ½" cubes
6 Garlic Cloves, peeled and sliced thin
½ teaspoon Pepperoncini (Red Pepper flakes)
1 – 28 can San Marzano Tomatoes
¼ cup fresh Basil
1 pound imported Italian Spaghetti
1/3 cup grated Pecorino Romano Cheese

Put olive oil and onions in a large 12 -14" frying pan and cook on low hear for 5 minutes while stirring.

Add the Zucchini and cook on medium heat for five minutes. Add Pepperoncini and garlic and cook on low heat for 3 minutes.

Add tomatoes. Turn heat to high and cook for three minute while stirring. Low heat to medium and cook 5 minutes. Lower heat to a low flame and cook for 12 minutes, stirring occasionally with a wooden spoon.

Tear Basil into smaller pieces with your hands (don't use a knife) and add to sauce pot. Cook on a low flame for 3 minutes. Turn heat off and let rest.

Cook the spaghetti according to the directions on package until al dente, about 10 minutes.
Drain the spaghetti in a colander, reserving a few tablespoons of water. Add the spaghetti back to the pot it cooked in. Sprinkle a bit of olive oil over the pasta and mix.

Add about a third of the Zucchini Sauce to the pot and mix with the spaghetti.

Plate the spaghetti on to 4-6 plates. Top each plate of pasta with a bit more sauce and sprinkle a tiny bit of olive oil over the pasta. Pass the grated Pecorino and enjoy.

SPAGHETTI con TONNO
alla PALERMITANO

This is a great Sicilian Pasta dish that you can whip up with ingredients that most Italian-Americans would always have in their cupboard, other than the fresh Parsley which may be omitted if you don't have any on hand. For this reason of all the ingredients being in the cupboard, my mother said that my nonna would make it every now in then. It's quick and easy to make, nutritious and you know it just has to be tasty.

RECIPE :

1 small Onion, peeled and minced fine
5 tablespoons Olive Oil
3 cloves Garlic, peeled & minced
½ teaspoon Red Pepper Flakes
3 Anchovy Filets, minced very fine
1 cup Italian Tomato Passata (thick tomato puree)
2 tablespoons Pine Nuts (optional)
3 tablespoons Gold Currants
12 ounces Italian Tuna packed in olive oil
¼ cup chopped fresh Italian Parsley
1 pound imported Italian Spaghetti
1/3 cup toasted Breadcrumbs

Place Olive Oil and onions in a medium sized frying pan or small pot. Cook over a low flame for 3 minutes.

Add minced Anchovies and garlic to pan and cook for two minutes on low heat, stirring with a wooden spoon as you cook. Add red pepper flakes and cook 1 minute. Add tomatoes, turn heat to high and cook for 3 minutes as you stir with a wooden spoon. Lower heat to low and let cook for 12 minutes, stirring occasionally.

As the sauce is simmering, put a large pot filled with four quarts of water on the stove to boil. Add 2 tablespoons of salt.

Break the tuna into smaller pieced, but try to keep intact and not broken too small (you want some whole chunks of tuna).

After to tomatoes have simmered for 12 minutes, add tuna to sauce with the Pine Nuts and Currants. Let cook on low heat for 2 minutes.

Cook the Spaghetti according to directions on package. When the spaghetti is finished cooking, drain it leaving about 5 tablespoon of water in the pot.

Add the spaghetti back to the pot it cooked in. Add 3 tablespoons of olive oil and half the parsley and mix. Add 1/3 of the sauce to the pasta and mix.

Plate the pasta among for plates in equal portions. Add remaining sauce in equal portions to the four plates of pasta. Sprinkle a little Parsley and some toasted breadcrumbs over each plate of pasta and serve to your guests.

LINGUINE con COZZE
Linguine with Mussels

We Italian-Americans love our Mussels, especially those who are of Neapolitan origins. Our favorite ways of eating them are; alla Marinara and Posillipo, and this one, made with either Spaghetti or Linguine, whichever pasta you may prefer. The dish will be equally tasty either way, and the mussels are much cheaper than clams. We love Clam Sauce, but the clams cost twice as much as the mussels do.

Ingredients :

2 pounds Prince Edward Island Mussels, cleaned
7 cloves Garlic, peeled and sliced fine
¼ cup Olive Oil, 1 teaspoon Red Pepper Flakes
3 cups Tomato Passata (crushed Tomatoes)
¼ cup fresh chopped Parsley
1 ½ cups water, 1 Bay Leaf
4 cloves Garlic, peeled and left whole
1 pound imported Italian Linguine or Spaghetti

Wash mussels and remove the beards (stringy thing protruding from the mussel) from the mussels. Place mussels in a large pot with the water, Bay Leaf, and 4 garlic cloves. Turn heat on high, and steam mussels until they all open (about 6 minutes). Remove from heat and let cool slightly.

Remove two-thirds of the mussels from pot and remove the mussels from the shells. Discard shells.

Place olive oil in a pan with sliced garlic and cook on low heat for minutes until the garlic starts to get slightly brown. Add red pepper and cook over very low heat for 1 minutes.

Add tomato passata to pan. Cook on medium heat for 12 minutes, stirring with a wooden spoon to keep from burning.

Cook pasta, following directions on box, this will take about 10 -12 minutes.

As the pasta is cooking add the mussels that you removed from shells to the tomato sauce and cook on very low heat for 4 minutes. Turn heat off after four minutes and let set.

Once the past has finished cooking, drain into a colander, reserving a ¼ cup of the pasta water.

Put the pasta back in the pot it cooked in with half the reserved cooking water. Add a drizzle of olive oil and mix. Add half the sauce and half the parsley to the pasta and mix.

Evenly divide the pasta with sauce among 4-6 plates, depending on how many people you want to serve.

Top each plate of pasta with a bit more sauce, and about 5 Mussels each that are still in the shell. Sprinkle a bit more Parsley and Olive Oil over the pasta and serve. Pass Red Pepper on the side for those who might like their pasta a bit spicy.

PASTA con SARDE

Pasta with Sardines

Pasta con Sarde is without question the single most popular savory dish in the Sicilian repertoire of food. Only Cannoli is a more famous and popular food. This is a dish that requires some practice and experimentation to get the dish just right. My grandmother made it to perfection. Her recipe follows below. This is one of the dishes, along with Spaghetti w/ Garlic Oil & Anchovies that is eaten most often on Saint Joseph's Day, one of the most important days of the Roman Catholic Season of Lent, and extra special to Sicilians. Eat these dishes on St. Joseph's Day, but they can be eaten any day of the year as they often are.

Grandma Bellino's Italian Cookbook

RECIPE:

¼ of a Fennel Bulb, cored and sliced fine
10 tablespoons Olive Oil
1 small Onion, peeled and sliced fine
4 cloves Garlic, peeled and minced
6 Anchovy Filets, minced
½ teaspoon Red Pepper Flakes
3 cans boneless skinless Sardines
¼ teaspoon each Sea Salt & Black Pepper
1 pinch of Saffron
3 tablespoons Golden Currants
3 tablespoons Pignoli Nuts, toasted
¼ cup fresh Parsley, washed, dried and chopped
1 pound imported Italian Bucatini, or Spaghetti
¼ cup plain Breadcrumbs, toasted

Put olive oil and fennel in a large frying pan and sauté on medium heat for 6 minutes. Add onions and cook on low heat for 7 minutes, stirring occasionally.

Add minced Anchovy and cook on medium heat for 4 minutes.

Add garlic and Red Pepper and cook on low heat for 3 minutes.

Add Sardines, Saffron, Currants and cook on low heat for 6 minutes. Be careful not to break the Sardine Filets to too much.

Cook pasta in rapidly boiling salted water according to directions on package. When pasta is finished cooking, remove from heat and drain in a colander reserving 6-8 tablespoons of water to add to sauce with the sardines.

Put the pasta back in the pot it cooked in. Add two thirds of the Parsley, half the Pignoli Nuts, and half the Sardine Sauce to the pasta and gently mix.

Evenly plate the pasta among 4 – 6 plates. Evenly distribute the remaining sauce over each plate of pasta. Sprinkle a little chopped Parsley and Pignoli Nuts over each plate of pasta and top each with the toasted breadcrumbs. Serve.

Grandma Bellino's Italian Cookbook

SAINT JOSEPH'S DAY PASTA

Saint Joseph's Day falls on March 19th and is also Fathers day in Italy. Saint Joseph was the Virgin Mary's husband and is the Patron Saint of Sicily. The day is quite important to Catholic Italians and especially those of Sicilian descent. New Orleans is the Sicilian-American enclave where they celebrate St. Joseph's Day more fervently than any other part of America, and they celebrate it in a big way. Most know Saint Joseph's Day Pasta as pasta with Garlic Oil & Anchovies with toasted breadcrumbs. This recipe is a bit different, but the one that my mother made and called St. Joseph's Day Pasta, so here it is. If you want to make the other one, use the previous recipe of Pasta con Aglio Olio e Acchiughe in this book. Just add toasted breadcrumbs to the recipe and you're all set.

RECIPE:

4 tablespoons Olive Oil
4 cloves Garlic, peeled and minced fine
¼ teaspoon Red Pepper Flakes
1 Bulb Fennel, cored & cut to 1 ½" pieces
1 small Onion, peeled and chopped
6 Anchovy Filets, minced fine
1 cup Tomato Passata (thick Tomato Puree)
12 fresh Basil Leaves, torn to a few pieces each
3 cans boneless skinless Sardines, drained
½ cup fresh chopped Parsley
1 pound imported Italian Percatelli
1/3 cup plain Breadcrumbs

Brown breadcrumbs in a frying pan with 2 tablespoons of olive oil until it is light golden brown. Set aside until later.

Drain Sardines of oil and set aside.

Place olive oil and chopped Fennel in a large frying pan and sauté on medium heat for 7 minutes. Add onions and cook on medium heat for 5 minutes.

Add Anchovies and cook on medium heat for 3 minutes.

Add garlic to pan with Red Pepper and sauté on low flame for 3 minutes.

Add tomato passata to pan. Cook on low heat for 14 minutes.

Add Golden Currants, half the Parsley, Basil, and Sardines and cook on low heat for 7 minutes more

Cook pasta following directions on package. When pasta is finished cooking, drain in colander, and reserve a few tablespoons of water.

Add pasta back to pot it cooked in, then add half the sauce and mix, being careful not to break-up the Sardines. Mix half the Parsley with breadcrumbs.

Plate pasta equally among 4 plates. Add a little more sauce to plated pasta. Sprinkle with breadcrumbs and serve.

LINGUINE with SHRIMP
alla UMBERTO'S

When I was in my late teens and early 20's, my friends and I would often go out for some late night eating after hitting our favorite bar. We'd either go to *Wo Hop's* for Chinese on Mott Street or *Umberto's Clam House* a few blocks away on Mulberry Street in New York's Little Italy, where we'd all get a plate of Linguine w/ Shrimp Marinara. My friend *Mike V* was the one who got us all going there as well as Wo Hop's, and we'd go there with Carlo Cavallo Richie & Jay Fahy and Jimmy Ryan.

Umberto's was a great lively restaurant that had a lot of energy and great food, including; Fried Calamari, Baked Clams, Clams on the ½ Shell, Spaghetti al Vongole, and their famed Linguine w/ Shrimps in either sweet, hot, or medium sauce. Back then, I usually got the sweet sauce, meaning that, it wasn't actually sweet, it's just that it had very little hot Red Pepper (Pepperoncino) in it. Medium sauce had a bit more hot pepper, enough to give it a little kick and make it a bit spicy but not too much, and the Hot Sauce had more Red Pepper flakes, making it hot. The recipe below is for the sweet sauce. If you want medium sauce put triple the amount of red pepper, and if you want it Hot, use 5 times as much of the Pepperoncino, as you like it, and enjoy.

RECIPE :

2 cups Tomato Passata
10 tablespoons olive oil
7 cloves of Garlic, peeled and sliced
½ teaspoon Red Pepper Flakes
10 fresh Basil Leaves, torn

1 ½ pound Shrimp, cleaned
1 pound imported Italian Linguine

Preparation :

Put half the olive oil in a pot with half the garlic and Red Pepper and cook on low heat for 3 minutes. Add tomato passata and Basil and cook on a low-medium simmer for 20 minutes.

Place remaining olive oil and garlic in a large frying pan with a pinch of Red Pepper flakes and cook on medium heat until you see the garlic just beginning to brown. When you do turn the heat up to high and quickly put the shrimp into the pan and cook on high heat until you see the shrimp is cooking towards the center but it will be raw on the top part. Turn heat off and turn over each piece of shrimps so they cook on the second side. Turn heat back to high and cook until second side of each shrimp is cooked through. This will take about 2 minutes.

Remove shrimp from heat and put into the tomato (marinara) sauce.

Cook the linguine in a large pot of salted rapidly boiling water according to the directions on the package, about 10 minutes.

Once the linguine is cooked, drain into a colander, reserving 4-5 tablespoons of pasta cooking water.

Put the linguine back in the pot it cooked in. Put half of the sauce over the past and mix.

Plate the linguine onto 4-6 plates, scrapping all the sauce out of pot onto the linguine. Top each plate of pasta with equal amounts of the remaining sauce, with equal amounts of shrimp for each person, and serve. Do not put and grated cheese on this sauce, "It's a No No."

MEZZE MONICA al CONTADINA
RIGATONI w/ MEAT SAUCE

This is what you might call the Sicilian version of the famed meat ragu from Emilia Romagna's the great Ragu alla Bolognese. Well it's not really a version of a Bolognese Sauce, as the Sicilians are not trying to copy a Bolognese Sauce. It's just how *we describe it to you here*. The main difference is that there is no wine in this Sicilian meat ragu, making it less rich than the Bolognese Ragu. Also this doesn't simmer as long as you do for the Bolognese, another factor of this *Peasant Dish*, as less cooking time is less money spent on fuel, and no wine in the sauce, makes it cheaper to prepare as well. Never-the-less, the dish is quite tasty, and one Grandma made often.

Ingredients:

1 pound Mezze Monica (half size Rigatoni)
6 links of Italian Sweet Sausage
1 small onion, peeled and minced
1 clove Garlic, peeled and minced fine
1 - 28 ounce can Crushed Tomato or Italian Passata di Pomodoro
4 tablespoons olive oil, Salt & Black Pepper
1 cup frozen Peas
6 tablespoons Heavy Cream (optional)
2 tablespoons butter, Grated Cheese

Place a large frying pan on top of the stove. Add the olive oil. Turn heat on to low. Remove the sausage meat from the skin and crumble into small pieces. Cook sausage meat on low heat for 8 minutes.

Add onions sauté for 6 minutes on low heat. Add the garlic, and cook two minutes.

Drain the oil off of the meat.

Add tomatoes, plus 1 cup of water to pan. Cook on high heat until the tomatoes come to the boil. Lower to a simmer and cook for 45 minutes, stirring sauce occasionally.

Add cream to pan and cook for 10 minutes. Add the frozen peas, cook 4 minutes on low heat. The Sauce is done.

Cook the Mezze Monica, (or other pasta) in rapidly boiling salted water. Cook according to directions on package.

Drain the pasta, reserving a few tablespoons of pasta cooking water. Put pasta and reserved water back in the pot the pasta cooked in. Add butter and mix. Add half the sauce to pot and mix. Serve pasta in equal portions on 4 plates. Top each plate of pasta with a large spoon of sauce. Pass around grated Pecorino or Parmigiano, and enjoy!

Note: Mezze Monica are short Rigatoni. You can use these or any other short pasta you choose for this dish. Spaghetti works well with it as well.

Grandma Bellino's Italian Cookbook

GRAVY

My grandmother simply called this tasty meat sauce *Gravy*. It's made with Veal Shank, chunks of pork shoulder, and Sweet Italian Sausages braised with a bit of wine and tomatoes. You need long slow cooking to get the meat tender, and you end up with a hearty, extremely tasty *Gravy* that everyone will love. All those except people who don't eat meat, or don't eat pork. Well, "Sorry for them," they don't know what they're missing! As for you, make it, serve it, and relish it!

1 Veal Shank
2 pounds Pork Shoulder Meat cut into 2" cubes
1 large Onion, peeled and minced
8 cloves Garlic, peeled and minced
2 carrots, peeled and minced fine
2 stalks Celery, washed & minced fine
¼ cup White Wine
6 – 28 ounce cans Crushed Tomatoes
3 tablespoons Tomato Paste
1 Bay Leaf, ½ a teaspoon Red Pepper Flakes
2 pounds Sweet Italian Sausages

Season the Veal Shank on both sides with salt & black pepper. Place half the Olive Oil in a 8-quart non-corrosive pot and brown the veal shanks on high heat until the veal is nice and golden brown on both sides, about 10-12 minutes. Remove from pot and set aside.
Season the Pork Shoulder meat with Salt & Pepper. Add Pork to the pot and brown over high heat in two separate batches.

Once all the meat is nicely browned, remove from pot and set aside. Add onions, celery, and garlic to pot and cook on low heat for 5 minutes.

Season the onions with a bit of salt & pepper. Add wine to pan and cook on high heat while scraping the bottom of the pan with a wooden spoon. This will dislodge and brown bits that have a lot of flavor from the bottom of the pan (deglazing). Cook until the wine is reduced by half its original volume.

Put all the Veal Shank & Pork back in the pot. Add crushed tomatoes, Bay Leaf, Red Pepper flakes, and tomato paste to pot. Fill an empty tomato can with water and put the water in the pot. Bring all to the boil, then lower flame to a low simmer.

Simmer for 2 hours 15 minutes, stirring and scrapping the bottom of the pan occasionally with a wooden spoon so the sauce doesn't stick.

After the sauce has been simmering for 90 minutes, brown the sausages in a pan with a little olive oil over medium heat until the sausages a lightly browned on all sides. Remove from pan and let cool for a few minutes.

Once the sausages are cooled, cut each link into 4 equal pieces each, then put into the sauce.

Remove the Veal Shank from the pot and let cool for a few minutes.

Once the veal has cooled enough to handle, remove the meat from the veal shank and break into pieces that are about 2" square. Put the veal meat back in the pot, and let everything simmer on low heat for another 45 minutes.

To Serve : Cook 1 or 2 pounds of your favorite maccheroni following the directions on the package. We like to use; Rigatoni, Mezze Monica, Cavatappi, Cavatelli, or any short maccheroni that you like.

When the pasta is ready (finished cooking), remove from heat, and drain in a colander, reserving ¼ cup or so of the pasta water to mix with the pasta and sauce. Put the pasta back in the pot it cooked in. Add some of the sauce with the pork and sausages to the pot. Drizzle a little olive oil over all and mix.

Spoon pasta onto however many plates you need. Top pasta with some more sauce on top and serve these glorious plates of food to your guest who should be salivating by now.

PS ... Make sure to have grated cheese on the table.

Grandma Bellino's Italian Cookbook

TIMBALLO di ANELLETTI
Grandma's Maccheroni Baked w/ Eggplant, Peas, and Sicilian Meat Ragu

Timballo is a supremely favorite dish of the Sicilian community. It is a special dish that is often served at large gathering like; Birthdays, Christening, and Weddings or for a small personal dinner parties. This recipe is my nonna's which is oh-so tasty, I'm sure you'll agree. My mother learned how to make it when she was a teenage girl and served it at family meals. This dish is especially suited to dinner parties as it's great for the host to make ahead. You can make everything for this Timballo ahead of time. A little before your guests arrive, you put the Timballo in the oven to cook. You can then relax with some wine and serve a salad or easy antipasto course while the Timballo is baking away in the oven. This dish is sure to please, in both taste and as a *discovery* of a *new dish* that most Americans have probably never had.

The RAGU :

1 medium Onion, peeled and chopped fine
2 Carrots, peeled and chopped fine
3 Garlic Cloves, peeled and minced
¼ cup Olive Oil
1 ½ pound Ground Beef, ½ cup dry Red Wine
1 -28 can crushed San Marzano Tomatoes
3 tablespoons Tomato Paste
1 cup water, 2 Bay Leaves
¾ teaspoon each of Sea Salt & Black Pepper

REMAINING INGREDIENTS :

2 medium Eggplants, un-peeled, cut into 1" cubes
½ cup Olive Oil
4 tablespoons Butter
10 oz. Button Mushrooms, cut in quarters
1- ¼ pound Caciocavallo Cheese
¼ cup grated Pecorino Romano Cheese
2 – 10 ounce boxes of frozen Peas
¾ teaspoon ground Cinnamon
½ cup dry Breadcrumbs
6 Hard Boiled Eggs, peeled and quartered
1 pound imported Italian Anelletti (aka Anellini)

To make the meat ragu, place the olive oil in a pot with the ground beef and cook on low heat while stirring with a wooden spoon until the meat loses its raw color. Add onions and continue cooking on low heat for 3 minutes. Add garlic and cook on low heat for 2 minutes.

Add wine and cook until the wine is reduced by half its original volume.

Add crushed tomatoes, tomato paste, bay leaf, and water to pot and bring up to the boil. Once all has come to the boil, lower heat and cook at a low to medium simmer for 1 hour & 25 minutes.

As the sauce is cooking, you will cook the mushrooms and eggplant.

Place remaining butter in a medium frying pan with 3 tablespoons of olive and cook on medium heat until the mushrooms are nicely browned, season with a little salt & black pepper and mix. Turn heat off and set aside.

Cook the eggplant in a large frying pan over high heat in separate batches. Do not stir so much, in order for the eggplant to brown, but you will be stirring it, just not too much. When each batch of eggplant is almost finished browning, season with a little salt & pepper lightly sprinkled over the eggplant, then remove from pan, and cook the next batch of eggplant.

Cook until all the eggplant is done, then set aside to later.

When the meat sauce is about 15 minutes away from being finished cooking, you will cook the Anelletti. Cook about 2 minutes less than called for on pasta package. Add the peas to the pasta, turn off heat and let sit 1 minute.

Drain the pasta & peas in a colander. Put the pasta & peas back in the pot it cooked in and sprinkle with a little olive oil. Add ¾ quarters of the meat ragu and half a teaspoon of the Cinnamon and mix.

Add the mushrooms and eggplant to pasta and mix.

Heat oven to 375 degrees. Grease a 10" spring form mold with butter. Add the remaining Cinnamon to the breadcrumbs and mix. Put breadcrumbs into the greased pan to coat it with the breadcrumbs.

Add the ¾ 's of the Caciocavallo Cheese to the pasta and mix.

Put half the pasta into the greased spring-form pan and press down slightly with the back of a wooden spoon. Arrange the hard cooked eggs in a nice circular pattern in the pasta and press each egg down into the pasta. Cover the eggs and pasta with the remaining Caciocavallo Cheese. Cover with the remaining pasta and press down slightly to fill pan completely.

Place in oven and cook at 375 degrees for 15 minutes. Lower heat to 350 and cook until the center is hot, about 30 minutes more. Turn heat off.

Remove the Timballo from oven and let set for 12-15 minutes before serving.

Scoop a good portion of the Timballo onto each guests plate. Drape each plate with about 3 tablespoons each of the reserved meat ragu, serve and pass around the grated Pecorino Romano.

LASAGNA CACATI

This dish originated from the town of Modica and the surrounding cities of Ragusa and Noto. Most every Sicilian just loves it, and it was a favorite of grandma Bellino, as it was for her children. My grandmother brought the recipe to Lodi, NJ and my mother learned to make it from her. I always loved this dish and started making it myself when I got older. Sicilians love to make jokes when giving names to some of there foods, like the Sicilian Potato Croquettes called Cazzilli (little Penis), and this dish whereby Cacati translates literally to Caca a.k.a. Poop. Don't let the name put you off. It's just a name and a little Sicilian humor. The dish is of course oh so tasty. If you don't want to call the dish Lasagna Cacati, you can call it Pasta al Forno alla Rugusana. Basta!

RECIPE :

2 pounds Sweet Italian Sausage
¼ cup Olive Oil
1 medium Onion, peeled and dice
5 cloves Garlic, peeled and sliced
½ teaspoon of Pepperoncino (Red Pepper flakes)
1/3 cup dry Red Wine
2 – 28 can San Marzano Tomatoes, chopped
4 tablespoons Tomato Paste
½ teaspoon each of Salt & Black Pepper
1 Bay Leaf

2 cups water
1 – 10 ounce box Frozen Peas
1 pound whole milk Ricotta Cheese
12 ounces grated Caciocavallo Cheese
2 lbs. Mafalde, (long curly Lasagna type pasta)
¼ cup grated Pecorino Romano Cheese

PREP :

Brown half the sausage links over low heat with a 2 tablespoons of olive oil in a 6 quart pot on medium heat until all sides of the sausages are lightly browned. Remove the sausage links from pan and set aside.

Remove meat from casings of remaining sausages and cook over low heat until the meat loses its raw color, about 5-6 minutes. Add onions and cook on low heat for 4 minutes.

Add wine and cook on medium heat until it is reduced by half its original volume, about 6 minutes.

Add remaining olive oil, red pepper flakes and garlic and cook on low heat for 4 minutes.

Add chopped tomatoes, slat & black Pepper, and turn heat up to high. Cook on high heat for 4 minutes while stirring.

Add water, tomato paste, and bay leaf and bring the liquid back to the boil. Turn flame down to a low simmer.

Cut the reserved sausage link into four equal pieces each and put in pot with sauce. Cook at a low simmer for 1 hour 15 minutes, stirring the bottom of the pot occasionally with a wooden spoon to prevent the sauce from sticking to the bottom of the pot.

When sauce (ragu) is almost finished cooking, cook the Mafalde pasta. Cook the Mafalde following the directions on the back of package, but cook for two minutes less than called for in directions as you will be baking the lasagna and it will cook more later on.

Drain pasta and return to the pot it cooked in. Drizzle a bit of olive oil onto the pasta and mix. Put a little more than 1/3 of the sauce into the pot with the pasta and mix. Add peas and mix.

Line the bottom of a shallow baking pan with a thin layer of sauce. Place half of the pasta in the pan. Take spoonful's of Ricotta and place dollops of it over the pasta. Cover with a thin layer of sauce, then cover this with half the grated Caciocavallo cheese.

Add remaining pasta to pan and spread out. Cover the pasta with remaining Caciocavallo. Cover this with half the remaining sauce. Bake in a 350 degree oven for 45 minutes.

Take Lasagna Cacati out of oven and let rest for 10 minutes before serving. Plate lasagna to each of your guest and pass around the grated Pecorino or any grated cheese you like. If you have some, sprinkle a little chopped fresh Parsley over each plate of Lasagna. Enjoy!

PASTA con SUGO di GALLINA
Grandma's Chicken Gravy Pasta

Most Americans might not think of Chicken Ragu as an Italian pasta sauce, but it is. This is a favorite of many Sicilian-Americans including our family. This is the recipe of Nonna Giuseppina Bellino.

RECIPE :

8 Chicken Thighs, ¼ cup Olive Oil
1 large Red Bell Pepper, cored and sliced
1 medium Onion, peeled and sliced
4 cloves Garlic, Peeled and minced
¼ cup dry White Wine
1/8 teaspoon each of Salt
Red & Black Pepper
1 – 28 oz. can Crushed Tomatoes
3 tablespoons Tomato Paste
1 pound Pasta (Rigatoni, Spaghetti)
10 ounces frozen Peas (optional)

Place half the Olive oil in a large frying pan with Bell Pepper and cook on medium heat for 8 minutes. Add onion and cook on low for 6 minutes. Season all with salt & Black Pepper, add garlic and cook 3 minutes.

Remove Pepper & Onions from pan and set aside.

Season Chicken with Salt & Pepper, add to pan with Olive Oil and cook on medium heat until the chicken is nicely browned, about 6 minutes on each side. Add wine and cook on high heat for 4 minutes.

Put chicken, Bell Pepper, and onion back to pan along with the tomatoes and tomato paste and turn heat to high. Bring to the boil. Once the liquid comes to the boil, lower heat to low and simmer until chicken is cooked through and tender, about 25 minutes. Add peas and let cook for 2 minutes.

Take the chicken out of pot, let cool, then remove chicken meat from the bones. Put chicken meat into pot with sauce & let cook on low heat for 7 minutes.

Cook the pasta according to directions on package. Drain pasta in colander when finished, then return it to the pot it cooked in along with about 6 tablespoons reserved pasta cooking water.

Add most of the Chicken Ragu to pasta and mix.

To serve, plate pasta with sauce onto 4-6 plates, drizzle with a little olive oil and top with some of the reserve Chicken Sauce.

Grandma Bellino's Italian Cookbook

LASAGNA CARNEVALE

Here's a Lasagna that few Americans have ever heard of, and even less have ever eaten it, including those of Italian ancestry. I myself didn't know about it until I was in my early 20's and was a cook at Ciao Bella Restorante on the UES of Manhattan. One of the Bus Boys who worked at the restaurant, who was from Napoli was talking about this dish one day and had me salivating. I'd never heard about it before, Lasagna with small Meatballs inside? I wanted it! I got the busboy Fabrizio to give me his mothers recipe, and I've been making it ever since. Little Kids especially love this Lasagna, mainly because of the little Meatballs inside. "Little Kids of all ages that is!"

RECIPE:

5- 6 cups Tomato Sauce
8 links Sweet Italian Sausages

MEATBALLS:

2 pound ground Beef
1 small Onion, minced fine
½ cup chopped fresh Parsley
½ teaspoon each Salt & Black Pepper
1 X-Large Egg, beaten
½ cup plain breadcrumbs
½ cup Milk

Remaining Ingredients :

1 ½ pound Mozzarella, grated
1/4 cup grated Pecorino Romano Cheese
2 pounds wide Lasagna noodles

Make tomato sauce from tomato sauce recipe in the beginning of this chapter.

Soak Breadcrumbs in the milk in a large glass mixing bowl for 10 minutes.

Add ground beef, Egg, salt & black pepper, to bowl with breadcrumbs and mix with your hands.

Add all but a few teaspoons of the Parsley to the meat. Add grated Pecorino Romano Cheese and mix with your hands.

Roll the ground meat mixture into little meatballs about the size of large marbles. Place the meatballs on a greased cookie sheet and bake in the oven at 350 degrees for 10 minutes. Remove meatballs from oven and let rest on the side.

Cook the Sausages in a medium sized frying pan with a little oil, over a medium flame until the sausages are nicely brown on all sides, about 7 minutes. Set aside to cool when done.

Cook the lasagna noodles in rapidly boiling salted water, according to the directions on package, but cook for 2 minutes less than the directions call for.

When finished, drain pasta in a colander, then run cold water over the pasta a couple minutes. Shake water off pasta and let set until needed.

Heat the tomato sauce on a medium flame for 10 minutes.

Cut the sausage links into ¼ " slices.

Coat the bottom of a shallow baking pan with some tomato sauce. Lay a layer of Lasagna Pasta over the tomato sauce to cover. Coat this layer of past with a little tomato sauce, then sprinkle on a light coating of grated Parmigiano over this. Put 1/3 of the meatballs on top of this layer, along with 1/3 the sausage slices and 1/4 of the grated Mozzarella. Repeat this step two more times.

Cover the top layer of Lasagna pasta with a light coating of tomato sauce, some grated Mozzarella and Parmigiano.

Turn oven on to 400 degrees and bake the Lasagna for 15 minutes. Turn the heat down to 350 degrees and bake about 35 minutes more until lasagna is hot in the center. Remove from oven and let set 12 minutes before cutting and serving.

Serve each person a nice square of Lasagna. Sprinkle a little Parsley over the top and pass some grated cheese. If you have some tomato sauce, pour a little strip over the top of the Lasagna before putting on the Parsley. Enjoy the fruits of your labor, along with your lucky guests.

MACCHERONI con SALSICCIA
Pasta with Sausage

This is a super simple pasta dish that is quick and easy to make. It's delicious and extremely satisfying, especially to Sicilians and other Southern Italians who love both their Sausage and Caciocavallo Cheese. The wonderful taste of the sauce is the purity of the sausage, devoid of any tomato at all. The dish takes just about 15 minutes to make, and you have a tasty meal that everyone will love, and who wouldn't love that, it's Maccheroni, Sausage, & Caciocavallo, all our favorites in one.

RECIPE :

1 pound Sweet Sausage
2 tablespoons Olive Oil, 1 tablespoon Butter
¼ cup fresh chopped Parsley
1/2 grated Caciocavallo Cheese
1 pound Cavatappi, Gemelli, or other pasta

Fill a large pot with boiling salted water for the pasta.

Remove sausage meat from casing and cook in olive oil in a pan over low heat until all the meat is cooked through and just slightly browned, about 10 minutes.

Cook the pasta according to directions on package. Drain pasta in colander reserving 5 tablespoons of the pasta cooking water. Place pasta back in the pot it cooked in with the reserved water, add butter and mix.

Drain half the oil from the sausages and place ¾ of the sausage in pot with pasta and mix. Add ¾ of the parsley and mix. Add half the cheese and mix.

To serve plate the pasta on 4-6 plates. Add a little of the remaining sausage meat to top of pasta and sprinkle with a little Parsley. Pass the grated cheese and enjoy.

Note: A 10 ounce box of frozen Peas is nice addition to this dish if you like. Also you can add 1 – ½ cups slice sautéed Mushrooms. The dish is wonderful on its own and really highlights the Sausage flavor as it is not diluted by cooking with tomatoes, which is perfectly fine, but a bit of another taste all-together as opposed to cooking the sausages basically on their own. However the peas and or mushrooms wouldn't really take away all that much of the flavor of the sausages, make it whichever way you like. Experiment, make the above recipe the first time, and then try it with mushrooms another time. Variety is the spice of life, so they say. It's oh so true. Enjoy!

ZITI con SUGO di AGNELLO
Pasta with Sicilian Lamb Ragu

Sicilian are quite fond of Lamb and this dish is the perfect example. Lamb wasn't that cheap, and making it into a meat ragu for pasta helps the meat go quite far as to how many people can be served. Two inexpensive Lamb Shanks can go a good long way. "Va Bene."

This recipe will serve about 6 portions, and you can even stretch it to 8 smaller pasta servings, and if you're having a salad or antipasto to start you can fill up a bit on that before moving on to the pasta.

RECIPE :

2 Lamb Shanks
2 Carrots, peeled and chopped fine
2 stalks Celery, washed and cut to small dice
1 medium Onion, peeled and chopped fine
4 cloves garlic, Peeled and chopped fine
¼ teaspoon each: Salt, Black Pepper, & Red Pepper
¼ cup dry Red Wine
1 – 28 ounce can crushed Italian Tomatoes
1 ½ cups water
2 bay Leafs
1 pound imported Italian Ziti (or Ronzoni)
½ cup fresh chopped Parsley

Season the Lamb Shanks with salt and black pepper and place in olive oil in a small non-corrosive pot. Brown the lamb on medium heat until it is nicely golden brown, about 12 minutes. Remove from pot and set aside.

Place Carrots & Celery in the pot and cook until lightly browned, about 8 minutes. Add onions and cook on low heat for 8 minutes with the carrots and celery.

Add garlic, salt, red pepper, and black pepper and cook on low heat for 3 minutes.

Add wine and cook on high heat until the wine is reduce by half, about 5-6 minutes.

Add tomatoes and bay leafs to pot. Add lamb back into pot with the water, and bring all up to the boil.

Once the liquid comes to the boil, lower flame so the liquid is at a low-medium simmer. Simmer until the lamb is tender, about 1 hour and 30 minutes. Remove the lamb and let cool a few minutes.

Once the lamb is cool enough to handle, remove the meat from the bone and add back to pot with the sauce (Gravy).

Let the lamb meat simmer at low heat for 15 minutes.

While the sauce is continuing to simmer, cook the pasta according to the directions on package. When the pasta has cooked, drain into a colander, reserving a ¼ cup pasta water. Put water into the sauce and mix.
Add the pasta back to the pot it cooked in. Sprinkle with a little Olive Oil and mix. Add half the Parsley and most of the sauce to the pasta, reserving a little sauce to garnish the top of pasta.

Plate the pasta onto 4-6 plates. Drizzle pasta with a little olive oil and chopped Parsley. Top each plate of pasta with a bit more sauce and serve.

RAGU alla SICILIANA
Sicilian Meat Ragu

This is one of my favorite Italian Meat Ragu's of all. It's an old Sicilian recipe that is full and hearty, which incorporates; Sausages, Pork Spare Ribs, and ground beef & pork. The meats are slowly braised with three aromatic vegetables and tomatoes to the end result of a lush robust *Soul Satisfy Gravy*. Cook up a batch and serve it with your favorite short pasta, such as; Rigatoni, Cavatappi, Ziti, or whatever pasta you like, this Sicilian Ragu *just can't be beat.*

RECIPE:

1/4 cup Olive Oil
2 Carrots, 2 Celery Stalks, cleaned and dice small
1 medium Onion, peeled and chopped fine
8 ounces each Ground Beef & Pork
10 Pork Spare Ribs
6 ounces Red Wine
12 Sweet Italian Pork Sausages
4 – 28 cans crushed Italian Tomatoes
2 Bay Leaf, 2 sprigs fresh Rosemary
1 teaspoon Crushed Red Pepper
1 teaspoon each Sea Salt & Black Pepper

Place olive oil in a large non-corrosive pot with the Celery & Carrots. Cook on medium heat for 5 minutes. Add onions, lower heat and cook at low heat for 5 minutes. Remove vegetables with a slotted spoon, leaving the oil in the pot. Set vegetables aside in a bowl to put in ragu later.

Cut Pork Ribs into individual pieces if they are not already this way. Season them with salt and pepper and put in pot to brown. Cook 4 minutes on each side over medium heat until slightly browned. Remove from pot and set aside with the vegetables.

Add ground beef and pork to pot, and season with a little salt & black pepper. Cook on medium heat for 5 minutes. Lower heat to low and cook about 4 minutes more until the ground meat losses its raw color.

Add wine and cook on medium heat until the wine is reduced by half, about 6-7 minutes.

Add tomatoes and bay leaf to pot and turn heat to high. Bring to the boil. Once all comes to the boil lower heat to a low simmer. Add Pork ribs and let simmer on low heat.

After the sauce has been simmering for 90 minutes, brown the sausages in pan on medium heat until all sides are lightly browned. Add to pot with sauce and let simmer for 45 minutes.

After the ragu has been simmering for a total of about 2 hours and fifteen minutes, add the Rosemary. Cook another 30 minutes on low heat. The ragu is finished. Turn the heat off and let set.

To serve, you can eat the ragu in one of two different ways. You can have it with the pasta in one course or you can serve a bit of the tomato sauce with pieces of ground meat with the pasta, reserving the Sausages and Pork Ribs and a little sauce to have as the main course with polenta or potatoes or some other vegetable of your choice.

When serving the ragu with some pasta, choose your favorite short maccheroni that is cooked according to the directions on package, dress with ragu and enjoy.

Grandma Bellino's Italian Cookbook

EGGPLANT PARMIGIANO

This recipe is from my dear Aunt Fran's who made the best Eggplant Parmigiano I've ever had anywhere, including numerous times all over Italy. Aunt Fran made me this dish many times over the years at her and Uncle Tony's house in Lodi. Often she'd make one of her tasty soups like Pasta & Peas, and if we were really lucky, Aunt Fran would have made her famous Ricotta Cookies as well, and we'd get to eat them for dessert, which was of course always a very special treat.

PS … Aunt Fran's Ricotta Cookie recipe is at the back of the book. What's better than that?

RECIPE :

7 cups Tomato Sauce (recipe in Book)
Salt & Black Pepper
2 cups Flour
4 Eggs
3 ½ cups plain Breadcrumbs
3 large Eggplants
12 fresh Basil Leaves, torn into pieces
2 ½ cups grated Parmigiano Reggiano
1 teaspoon each Sea Salt & Black Pepper
2 cups Vegetable Oil for Frying Eggplant

Place flour in a shallow dish with half the salt & half the black pepper. Add remaining salt & pepper to the eggs and together in another shallow dish. Mix breadcrumbs with a pinch of salt & pepper in a third shallow dish. Set dishes aside.

Peel and trim eggplant and slice across the width into slices that are in-between ¼" and ½" thick. Dredge each slice first in the flour, then in the egg, then in the seasoned breadcrumbs, until all of the eggplant slices are coated with breadcrumbs.

Put oil in a large frying pan, and heat to medium-high heat until oil is hot but not smoking. Add breaded eggplant slices to the hot oil (work in batches, if needed) and cook until golden on both sides and dark brown on the edges, 2 -3 minutes per-side. Fry all the breaded eggplant slices.

Spread a thin layer of tomato sauce in the bottom of a large shallow ovenproof dish. Arrange eggplant in a single layer on top of tomato sauce. Sprinkle with Parmigiano Reggiano, a quarter of the Parmigiano. Repeat this step until you have about 3 layers of eggplant.

Bake in a 375 degree oven for 15 minutes. Turn heat down to 350 and bake another 30 minutes.

Remove Eggplant from oven and let stand for 10 minutes before serving. Most people eat Eggplant Parmigiano as a main-course, but it's also great as an Antipasto item, whereby you will serve a portion 1/3 to half the size of a main-course. Buon Appetito!

STUFFED PEPPERS alla LUCIA

These Stuffed Peppers where one of my mother's best dishes. They're easy to make, and as with many Sicilian-American dishes of the early 20th Century, they are quite inexpensive to make, as the ground beef is relatively cheap, and the rice that goes in the stuffing with the beef, stretches the beef out further, so it goes a long way. These stuffed peppers are a great make ahead meal. We most often ate this dish as a main course, but in Italian-American restaurants it's popular antipasto item on its own or as part of a mixed antipasti along with Eggplant Rolitina and Baked Clams

RECIPE :

1 medium onion, minced
3 cloves of garlic, minced
6 Tablespoons chopped parsley
6 Tablespoons bread crumbs
2 eggs. Salt & Pepper
1 cup long grain rice
¾ lb. ground pork, ¾ lb. ground beef
1 Tablespoon Dry Oregano
½ cup grated Pecorino Romano
4 Red or Green bell peppers
½ cup chicken broth
1-1/2 cups tomato sauce

Preparation for Lucia's Stuffed Peppers:

Cook the rice for 12 minutes in boiling water and drain.

Cut the tops off the peppers and reserve.

Mix all remaining ingredients except the Broth and sauce in a large bowl.

Stuff the peppers with the meat mixture and top with the Pepper tops.

Place the peppers in a small baking pan with the broth. Cover with aluminum foil. Bake at 350 for 40 minutes. Remove foil and continue Baking for 15 minutes longer.

Heat the tomato sauce. Put 6 Tbs. of sauce on a plate with a pepper.

Serve with grated cheese.

RISO con CUCUZZA e CARNI
Rice with Gagootz !!!

Rice & Gagootz? Well, Rice, Cucuzza, & Beef that is. This dish is from inland Sicily in the towns of; Corleone, Lercara Friddi, Prizzi, and *Salemi*, my grandmothers namesake town. The dish is extremely authentic Sicilian and not well know in this country. We Bellino's know it well as my Nonna Giuseppina made it for my mother, and my mother made it for me and my brothers Jimmy and Michael and sister Barbara. The dish is inexpensive, easy to make, and will feed at least eight hungry people. We Sicilians love our *Gagootza* of which this dish features along with beef, tomatoes, and rice.

This dish is not a soup, but can be made into a soup, simply by adding a little water to the tomatoes and beef when cooking or when you are heating up any leftovers the next day

If when you make this dish, and four people or less are eating it, you will have some leftover for the next day or following day, whereby we usually serve it as a soup. And if you need to stretch the leftovers out a bit, you can add a can of cannellini or other beans to it, or some boiled potatoes help the dish to go a long way, and that's thrifty Sicilian cooking for you.

RECIPE :

1 medium sized Cucuzza (Gagootz)
¼ cup Olive Oil
1 large Onion, peeled and diced
4 cloves Garlic, peeled and sliced
1 pound ground Beef
1 -28 can San Marzano Tomatoes
½ teaspoon Pepperoncino (Red Pepper flakes)
2 cups long grain Rice, washed
1 tablespoon Butter
1 teaspoon Sea Salt, ½ teaspoon Black Pepper

Peel the cucuzza, and cut into 1½ inch cubes. Set aside.

Add olive oil and onions to a large pot and cook on low heat for 5 minutes. Add garlic and cook on low heat for 2 minutes while stirring with a wooden spoon.

Add ground beef and cook on low heat while stirring until the beef loses its raw color. Add half the Salt and all the black pepper and cook on low heat for 1 minute.

Drain tomatoes, reserving the juices. Put tomatoes and red pepper flakes in pan and turn the heat to high. Cook for three minutes while stirring. Add the reserved tomato juices and the Cucuzza, and continue cooking on high heat until it all comes to the boil.

Add Bay Leaf, lower heat so all is at a low to medium simmer. Cook at a simmer for about 25 minutes.

As the Cucuzza & Beef are cooking, start the rice. Add the rice with 4 cups of water, half the salt, and butter to a small pot. Bring to the boil. Once all the liquid comes to a boil, lower heat to the lowest the flame will go, and let cook for 15 minutes uncovered. After 15 minutes, turn the heat off, cover the pot and let sit for 5 minutes before serving.

To serve the dish, take a coffee cup and fill it with rice, pressing the rice into the cup. Place this in a shallow pasta bowl, shake and remove cup, leaving a mound of rice that has the shape of the cup. Take the Cucuzza & Beef and spoon a good amount into the bowl surround the rice.

Drizzle a little Olive Oil over the top and pass around a bit of your favorite grated cheese, Pecorino Romano, Caciocavallo, Parmigiano, or whatever you like.

NOTE: If you can't get a Cucuzza, or if you prefer, you can substitute Zucchini for the Cucuzza. Either way, this dish is equally excellent.

CAN'T FIND GAGOOTZ ????

Buy it mail order from Cordaro Cucuzza Plantaion 718 West Tennessee Ave.Ruston, LA 71270

http://www.cucuzzasquash.com/index.html

Grandma Bellino's Italian Cookbook

PESCE

Fish? As far as fish is concerned with Italian-Americans, for the majority, it's Clams first. Clams in the form of Baked Clams, Clams Posillipo, and of course we have to have our favorite, Spaghetti al Vongole, aka Spaghetti with Clam Sauce. Also, we love our Mussels in Mussels Marinara, or Posillipo, and with Spaghetti as well. Some of us love Octopus, others don't, and of course there's Fried Calamari which everyone loves. And don't forget Shrimp in the forms of; Shrimp Marinara, Shrimp Oreganata, and the much loved Shrimp Fra Diavolo. When it comes to actual Fish other than Shellfish, our favorites are Bacala (Cod), Tuna, Swordfish, and Filet of Sole.

Now, as it concerns the Sicilians in Sicily it is natural that they are great lovers of fish, as it is that they are surrounded by the Sea on all sides. Yes, they're great fish lovers, but that wasn't always the case with all Sicilians, as was the case with my own maternal grandparents Giuseppina and Philipo Bellino. When they were still living in Sicily in Lercara Friddi in the 1880's & 90's, fish was not greatly prevalent. They lived just 45 kilometers from the sea, but with no refrigeration and just horse and donkey carts to transport things, they might have well have been a thousand miles away. Yes they ate fish, but not a lot. They had their soups and pasta, but apart from these, they ate more meat than fish, and when they did have fish it was mostly in the form of cured fish, like

Bacala, Preserved Tuna, Anchovies, and Sardines. When my grandparents moved to America, they started eating a bit more fish, but never became big fish lovers, though they did like having some now and then. That's the story of fish and my maternal grandparents. We the younger generations, my mother and her sister and brothers ate a bit more fish, and the next generation; my sister, brothers, and cousins, we eat quite a bit more than both our parents and grandparents. Basta!

PESCE SPADA alla MESSINESE
Swordfish in The Style of Messina

The great spectacle of the Mattanza when Tuna run through the Straits of Messina is legendary. These straits are the body of water that separates Sicily from mainland Italy. There is an abundance of both Tuna & Swordfish surrounding the waters of Sicily, so for this reason Swordfish and Tuna (Tonno) are the two most popular fish of the city of the coastal city of Messina and all of Sicily for that matter. This is a tasty dish that features this favorite Sicilian fish, along with some of its other favorite Sicilian ingredients of; Capers, Anchovies, Oregano, & Olives, so enjoy.

RECIPE :

4 fresh Swordfish Steaks, about 7 ounces each
Sea Salt & Black Pepper
¼ cup Olive Oil
1 small Onion, peeled and sliced thin
3 Anchovy Filets, minced
2 cloves Garlic, Peeled and minced
2 pieces Roast Red Pepper from a jar, chopped
4 tablespoons Raisons, soak 15 minutes in hot water
3 tablespoon Pignoli Nuts
1 teaspoon dry Oregano
3 tablespoons Sicilian Capers
¼ cup small Green Olives, pits removed
¼ cup chopped fresh Parsley
1 Lemon, cut in 4 quarter pieces

Place Olive Oil, onions, and Anchovies in a medium frying pan and cook over medium heat for 4 minutes.

Add Garlic, Roast Red Pepper, and Pignoli Nuts to pan and cook on medium heat for 3 minutes.

Soak the Raisons in hot water to get plump, then drain. Add Raisons, Oregano, Capers, and Green Olives to pan and mix. Turn off heat and set aside.

Season both sides of each piece of Swordfish with salt and black pepper to taste. Cook the swordfish pieces in a large frying pan coated with a little olive oil at high heat for 3 minutes on each side.

Place each cooked piece of Swordfish on a plate. Garnish with a piece of Lemon.

Mix the Parsley in the pan with the sauce, and spread equal portions of the sauce over each Swordfish.

Serve with whatever vegetable you like on the side; Sautéed Broccoli Rabe, Caponata, Roast Potatoes, or whatever you like.

PESCE alla LUCIA
Jersey Bluefish in The Style of My Mother Lucia Bellino

When we were kids growing up in New Jersey, we had a few neighbors that would go fishing down the Shore. "Down The Shore," that's the way Jerseyites describe going to the beach, aka *Seashore*. . A couple of our neighbor friends would go Crabbing or fishing on what they call Party-Boats (large Sport Fishing Boats) that run down-out of Pt. Pleasant, Belmar, and other Jersey Shore points. In the Summer, when Bluefish & Mackerel were running up the Jersey Shore the catch was always quite abundant. Our fishermen friends would come back with a bountiful catches, especially with Mackerel of which they might catch up to 100 fish each. Bluefish are a bit different. They are much larger, and there's no way of bringing back 100 Bluefish, as is the case with Mackerel. Nevertheless a few Bluefish was a good catch and more than they needed or could eat, so the local gentlemen fishermen would always give my mom some nice freshly caught fish from the Jersey Shore, and one large Bluefish could feed the whole family. The following is my mom's recipe for cooking the *gifted* Bluefish, whenever she was lucky enough to get some.

RECIPE:

4 Bluefish Filets 7-8 ounces each
1/3 cup Olive Oil
Sea Salt & Black Pepper
1 cup Tomato Sauce
3 cloves Garlic, peeled and sliced
3 Anchovy Filets, minced
4 tablespoons Capers
¼ cup small Black Olives, pits removed
¼ cup fresh chopped Parsley

Place a thin film of olive oil in a medium sized glass or ceramic baking dish. Add the bluefish to the pan. Sprinkle with a little Sea Salt & Black Pepper, and drizzle with olive oil.

Bake the Bluefish in a 350 degree oven until they are cooked through to the center, about 16 minutes.

Make the sauce by putting the remaining olive oil in a small frying pan with the garlic and anchovies. Cook on medium heat for 3 minutes.

Add tomato sauce to pan with the Olives, Capers, and add half the Parsley. Cook 5 minutes on medium heat.

Remove Bluefish from the oven and let rest for 5 minutes before serving. Plate the fish onto 4 plates with a quarter slice of Lemon each.

Pour a little sauce over each fish, and sprinkle with Parsley. Serve with whatever vegetable you like and enjoy.

PESCE alla SICILIANA
Fish Cooked Sicilian Style

This method of cooking fish is the preferred Sicilian way to cook fish. It's simple, tasty, and quite popular to cook Swordfish this way, and when the Sicilian immigrants like my Nonna Giuseppina came to America, she'd cook the local East Coast Fish like Cod, Grouper, & Pollack in this manner. So, get whatever fish you like; Bluefish, Cod, Haddock, and or Grouper are all great, as is that very Sicilian fish we call Swordfish. This method also works well with Jumbo Shrimp, of which Italian-Americans are quite fond of.

RECIPE :

4 – 8 oz. Filets Fresh Cod, Grouper, or Pollack
1/3 cup Olive Oil
Juice of 1 Lemon and 1 Lemon cut into 4 wedges
1 teaspoon dry Oregano
2 cloves Garlic, peeled and minced
1 cup plain dry Breadcrumbs
¼ teaspoon each Sea Salt & Black Pepper
¼ cup chopped fresh Parsley

Coat a small glass-baking-pan with four tablespoons Olive Oil.

Place all remaining ingredients except for the fish and half the Parsley in a glass bowl and mix. Turn oven on to 375 degrees.

Sprinkle both sides of the fish with a little salt & pepper.

One at a time, take a piece of fish and put into the bowl with the breadcrumbs and press breadcrumbs into the bottom and top of the fish. Do this for all 4 pieces of fish, and lay them in the oiled baking pan, skin-side down.

Bake in the oven until the fish are cooked through in the middle, about 12-15 minutes depending on the thickness of the filets.

The best way to check if the fish is done, is by piercing the very center of the fish with a small sharp knife and look inside. If the fish is still a little raw, you know you'll have to cook it a few more minutes. If it is not raw in the center, it's done. You can use this method of checking with anything you cook; fish, meat, or poultry.

When the fish is done cooking, take out of the oven and let it rest for 3 minutes before serving. Put one piece of fish with a wedge of lemon on each plate along with some boiled or roast potatoes or some niece green vegetable recipe from this book. Buon Appetito!

MUSSELS MARINARA

"Mommy's Favorite"

Mussels Marinara, Mommy's favorite! It certainly was, as it is for millions of Italian-Americans across the country, especially those of Neapolitan Ancestry. The dish is at its height in Naples, Italy (Napoli) and its environs, like; Capri, Ischia, Positano, Amalfi, and Puzzuolli the birthplace of Sophia Loren. In America the dish is most often eaten as an appetizer, whereby in Naples, it is more often eaten as a main-course. No matter, it's great to have either way. And make sure you have a nice loaf of Italian Bread to sop up any Sauce after you're done when all the Mussels are gone, you've still got bread and sauce.

INGREDIENTS:

3 lbs. Prince Edward Island Mussels, cleaned
6 cloves of Garlic, peeled and sliced thin
7 tablespoons Olive Oil
Pinch of Pepperoncino (Red Pepper Flakes)
¼ cup White Wine
1 ½ cup water
3 ½ cups Tomato Sauce
¼ Fresh Chopped Italian Parsley

In a small pan, Sauté Garlic in Olive Oil over medium heat for 4 minutes. Add red pepper flakes and cook 30 seconds more.

Put white wine in a pot large enough to hold all of the Mussels. Turn on heat to high, and cook until wine is reduced by half, about 5 minutes. Add mussels and water and cover. Cook over high heat until all the mussels open. You will have to stir with a large spoon to or 3 times to move the mussels around. Keep the pot covered so the mussels will steam. When just about all the mussels have opened, turn off heat. Discard any mussels that have not opened.

When the mussels are cooking, add tomato sauce to pan with garlic and olive oil. Turn heat on to medium and cook about 6 minutes.

Once the mussels are all cooked and you have discarded any mussels that did not open, remove Mussels from pot and place in a large serving bowl or individual serving bowls.

Pour the mussel cooking-liquid in the pan with the Marinara Sauce and heat over medium heat while stirring for five minutes.

Pour Sauce over Mussels and serve with toasted Italian Bread.

GAMBERONI con AGLIO OLIO
Shrimp with Garlic & Oil

RECIPE:

1 – ½ lbs. large size Shrimp, shelled and deveined
¼ cup Olive Oil
8 cloves Garlic, peeled and sliced
¼ teaspoon Pepperoncino (Red Pepper Flakes)
Sea Salt & Black Pepper

Clean the shrimp by removing the shell, leaving the tail still attached. Remove the black vein down the center of each shrimp. Wash in water, then pat dry.

Cook the shrimp in two batches. Place olive oil and garlic in medium pan and cook on low heat until garlic just starts to turn brown on the edges. Add the red pepper, and quickly turn heat to high.

Add half the shrimp and cook on high heat until you see the shrimp almost cooked toward the center of the side it is cooking on. Quickly turn all the shrimp over and cook on 2nd side until the shrimp just lose all the rawness throughout. Remove shrimp from pan and set aside.

Add the rest of the shrimp and repeat the cooking process as for the first batch.

Serve equal amounts of Shrimp and the sauce on 3 or 4 plates along with your favorite vegetable. Green Beans and or boiled potatoes or a mix salad all go well with these shrimp.

Grandma Bellino's Italian Cookbook

CARNI e GALLINA

Carni e Gallina, that's Meat & Chicken. As I've already stated, years ago, Sicilians living inland in Sicily, though on an island that is surrounded by the sea, did not have a readily accessible supply of a lot of fish, especially fresh fish. As a result, they ate more poultry and meat than fish, and thus our family along with many other Italian-Americans do eat our fare share of meat and poultry. You know we love our Sausages & Braciole, Chicken Cacciatore, Pork Chops, Chicken Cutlets, Veal Milanese & Marsala, Steaks, Lamb, Rabbit, and more. In Palermo and other parts of the island of Sicily they love their wonderful sandwiches, one of which is known as a Vestedda made with Beef Spleen, Ricotta, and Caciocavallo Cheese, it's my very own all-time favorite sandwich.

Meat was always big in our house and especially with my Uncles Frank & Tony, who believe it or not weren't the biggest pasta lovers as a result of having to eat it everyday of their young lives. Yes, when we had our Sunday Meals at Aunt Helen's or over Uncle Tony's house, often we'd have meat or Uncle Frank's favorite of all, Chicken Cacciatore. Meat? We'd have the Sunday Sauce Gravy, or simply some Spaghetti & Meatballs, Sausage & Peppers, or one of Tony's special roasts, or his most famous dish of all, Veal Marsala alla Tony.

My Uncles loved roast meats with some carrots and potatoes. Uncle Tony might roast some Pork, Beef, or Lamb, which could be proceeded with one of Aunt Fran's tasty soups of Pasta & Peas, or Escarole & Beans, but never Lentils as Uncle Frank just would not have it. Yes we love our meat, but we eat a bit more healthy these days. There will always be lots of good healthy green vegetables, like; Green Beans, Scarola, Broccoli Rabe, and salad. We do love our meat, but we eat quite a bit more fish then our grandparents did, who didn't eat it as much, simply because it wasn't available and the fact that it was more expensive than meat. So here follows some meat, poultry, and rabbit recipes from my Nonna and other Bellino Family members as well.

PUTINE di MAILE con SALSICCE
Spare Ribs & Sausage

This dish from the southern Sicilian City of Ragusa and is as tasty as can be. Just imagine, a sauce that features Italian Sausages and succulent Pork Spare Ribs? Believe me, it doesn't get much better than this. I know all you Italian guys feel the same way, excited at the thought of it. If you've never had Italian Style Spare Ribs that have been slowly braised with tomatoes and aromatic vegetables, then you're in for a treat. Normally this dish is eaten as a two-course meal. You make the gravy, and when it's done, you take some of the sauce (minus any meat) from the pot and serve it dressed over whatever pasta you choose to make. After you have the maccheroni, you eat the Sausage & Ribs for the main-course, along with some roast or boiled potatoes.

My friend Francesca Planeta and her family have their renowned winery, *Planeta* down outside of the city of Ragusa, and I recommend drinking their Nero d'Avola or Cerasuolo di Vittoria to go along with this tasty maccheroni and ragu, it's a pairing made in heaven. Do it!

REICPE :

3 pounds pork Spare Ribs
2 pounds Italian Sweet Sausage (or Hot if you like)
1 medium Onion, peeled and chopped fine
8 cloves of Garlic, peeled and sliced thin
4 – 28 cans San Marzano Tomatoes, chopped
5 tables spoons Tomato Paste
1 teaspoon Pepperoncino (Red Pepper Flakes)
1 teaspoon Salt & 1 teaspoon Black Pepper
1 cup Red Wine, 2 Bay Leaves, 1 pound Rigatoni

Cut pork spare ribs into individual pieces of 1 or 2 ribs each.

Place olive oil and onions in a 8 quart pot. Cook on low heat for 5 minutes.

Add garlic and red pepper flakes and cook on low heat for 5 minutes.

Drain the tomatoes from cans, reserving the juices. Chop tomatoes and place in pot with tomato paste. Cook on high heat for 5 minutes while stirring with a wooden spoon.

Add tomato juices and three cups water. Bring to the boil, and then lower to a simmer.

As the tomatoes are simmering, cook the ribs in olive oil in a large frying pan. Season the ribs with salt & black pepper and cook on high heat, browning the ribs nicely on all sides. Cook the ribs in 2 or 3

batches. When each rib is nicely brown, add to pot with tomatoes.
You will be simmering the ribs until nice and tender, about 90 minutes to 1 hour and 45 minutes.

After the ribs have been simmering for about 35 minutes, lightly brown all the sausages in the same pan you brown the ribs in. Once finished browning, remove from pan and let cool a few minutes.

Once the sausages are cool enough to handle, cut each link into 3 pieces each, then put in pot to cook with the ribs.

Cut up cook (Boil) 2 or 3 potatoes that you will serve with the Ribs & Sausages as the main-course.

Cook ¾ of a pound of Rigatoni according to directions on package (about 11 minutes). When pasta is finished cooking, drain in a colander.

Return Rigatoni to the pot it cooked in, and add some of the tomato sauce to the pot along with a drizzle of Olive Oil, and mix.

Plate the Rigatoni onto plates, drizzle on some Olive Oil and pass some grated cheese.

When finished eating the Maccheroni, you will then move on to the meat.

Serve each person 4-5 Spare Ribs each and a few pieces of Sausages each, along with a few pieces of boiled potatoes or polenta. Sprinkle with chopped Parsley if you have it, and Enjoy the succulence. It's absolutely sublime!

Grandma Bellino's Italian Cookbook

BRACIOLE

Braciole? Here's another one of the most beloved and popular of all of the great dishes of the Italian-American Table, *Braciole*. In the realm of popularity, Braciole ranks 5th after Spaghetti Pomodoro, Pizza, Meatballs, and Sausage. And to some Braciole is their absolute # 1 *favorite*, while others, not, it all depends on the person and their own personal preferences. All we can say is Braciole is way up there.

Still to this day years later, I can see my mom making Braciole; seasoning the meat, stuffing it, rolling it up, tying it, then adding to a pot of tomato sauce for a long slow braise before emerging from the pot and the sauce that it has flavored. The Braciole is tasty and succulent and always a great treat. You can make Braciole on its own then serving it with pasta, potatoes, or polenta, commandeering some of the sauce to coat some pasta as a course before the Braciole, and have the Braciola as the main course with potatoes or Polenta afterwards. Yes you can make the Braciole on its own, or you can of course include it in the most supreme of all Italian-American dishes, Sunday Sauce Gravy, along with Meatballs and Sausage for one of the world's tastiest dishes of all, Sunday Sauce.

RECIPE: BRACIOLE

SAUCE For The BRACIOLE

3 - 28 oz. cans San Marzano crushed tomatoes
or other good quality Italian style tomatoes
7 cloves minced garlic
1 small onion, minced
½ teaspoon crushed red pepper
¼ cup virgin olive oil
¼ cup chopped fresh basil or 1 tsp. dried
Salt and pepper to taste

In a 6 quart or larger pot, sauté onions over a low flame for 3 minutes. Add garlic and cook for 3-4 minutes. Do not let the garlic get dark or burn.

Add tomatoes, turn heat up to high and stir. When sauce starts to bubble, turn flame down so the sauce is at a low simmer. Simmer for 20 minutes before adding the Braciole.

For The BRACIOLE

1 - 1/2 pounds Beef Flank Steak (cut the beef on an angle in pieces approximately 3 ½" by 6 ½")
6 cloves garlic, peeled and chopped..
½ cup fresh Italian parsley, washed,
dried and chopped
¼ Cup Grated Pecorino Romano Cheese
¼ cup Bread Crumbs, plain
Olive Oil, Raisons, Sea Salt & Black Pepper

Once the beef has been cut, lay all the pieces out on a clean table. Lightly season the beef with salt & pepper.

Drizzle a little olive oil over each piece of beef. Evenly distribute chopped Parsley over all the Beef.

Evenly distribute the Pecorino Cheese over all the beef.

Sprinkle Bread Crumbs over Beef. Put to raisons on to each slice of Beef.

Roll each piece of beef Jelly-Roll style. Take two toothpicks for each piece of beef and fasten each piece of beef closed with the toothpicks.

Lightly salt & pepper the outside of each rolled piece of beef.

Brown all the Beef Rolls (Braciole) in a pan with Olive Oil. Once all the beef is nicely browned, put all the Beef Braciole into tomato sauce or meat gravy that you have already started. Tomato Sauce recipe follows.

Cook the Braciole on a low flame until the Braciole are tender, about 1 hour and 45 minutes.

Grandma Bellino's Italian Cookbook

SUNDAY GRAVY

Gravy, a.k.a. Sunday Sauce, Sunday Gravy, and simply *Sauce*. What do you call it? You know, whether you call it Sunday Sauce or Gravy, it's the most-supreme dish of all of this great food loving community we call Italian-America. There are any number of ways to make this great dish, and different recipes as you've already seen from my grandma's Gravy on page 158, that doesn't have Braciole or Meatballs in it, she usually made the Meatballs for Spaghetti & Meatballs and the Braciole on their own as separate dishes. However, many, or most make their Sunday Gravy with Meatballs, Sausage, and maybe Braciole. If you want to make some *Gravy* this way, simply, *make* the *Braciola recipe above,* make a batch of Meatballs from the Spaghetti & Meatball recipe previously in the book, and after the Braciole has been cooking for 1 hour, add 1- ½ lbs. of browned sausages and simmer them along with a batch of meatballs and cook for another 45 minutes and you've got yourself some Sunday Sauce, otherwise known as *Gravy.* This is the most popular version that is made with Sausage, Meatballs, and Braciole. Yes this is Gravy a.k.a. Sunday Sauce, or Sunday Gravy. Make this dish and you and yours will be in *Culinary Heaven,* I *guarantee* !!!

CHICKEN CACCIATORE

Chicken Cacciatore has long been a mainstay of the Italian-American table. Made with chicken, which many Italian immigrants hardly ever ate in Italy as it was so expensive there. These same Italian immigrants couldn't believe their good fortune of such low prices for meat and poultry in their adopted homeland, America. Chicken along with beef and pork was very affordable and might find its way to these immigrants tables once or twice a week or more, and especially in the from of the much loved Chicken Cacciatore, Broiled Chicken, Roast Chicken, and Chicken Scarpariello as well. This is my grandmother Giuseppina's recipe for Cacciatore.

RECIPE :

1 whole broiler chicken cut into 10 pieces, 2 wings, 2 thighs, 2 legs, and 2 Breast cut in 4 pieces
1 medium onion, peeled and diced
6 cloves of Garlic, peeled and sliced
1 can of whole San Marzano Tomatoes
¼ teaspoon Red Pepper Flakes
Sea Salt & Black Pepper

Season chicken with salt & pepper. Cook chicken in a large frying pan over high heat until all of the chicken is nicely browned. About 12 minutes.

Add onions, cook for 5 minutes. Add garlic, cook for 2 minutes.

Turn heat to high, add tomatoes. Cook for 2 minutes at high heat. Season with Salt & Black Pepper, then lower heat to low, and simmer for 20 minutes. Serve with boiled potatoes or whatever vegetable you like.

Note: When browning the chicken, it is very important to get the chicken nice and brown. In browning the chicken as in any dish where you are browning poultry, or meat, the browning is caramelizing the meat and brings an abundance of flavor to it, as well as properly seasoning with salt & pepper, so make sure you do a good job and get the chicken nice and brown before it cooks with the tomatoes, onion, and peppers. Once the chicken goes in with the remaining ingredients it will no longer be able to brown.

NOTE II: This is my grandmother's recipe and stays as is with not alterations. It's very simple. If you'd like to change this recipe around a little, you can do so, as you can do with most any recipes. One way of making the dish is add either some Mushrooms or Red Bell Peppers to the dish. Those Italian Americans whose families come from the north might be more apt to add mushrooms, while southerners would add the bell peppers. You can also add a little red or white wine to the dish at the step after you brown the chicken and before you add the tomatoes.

POLLO SCARPAREILLO

Grandpa Bellino's Shoemaker Chicken

Chicken Scarpariello, "Shoemakers Chicken. "That's what my Grandfather Philipo was, a shoemaker from Lercara Friddi, Sicily, the same town that the great Frank Sinatra's father Anthony Martino Sinatra was from, and Sinatra's grandfather was a Shoemaker from Lercara Friddi as well. My Mother's Father Philipo Bellino and Mother Giuseppina immigrated to the United States through the Port of New York at Ellis Island in 1904. My Grandfather Philipo Bellino opened a shoemaker shop on Main Street, in Lodi, New Jersey (Soprano Territory).

Like most dishes, there are different variations on the theme. There are different ways to make this dish, but the two main differences are that one is made with sausages, and one without. Being Sicilian, my grandfather Philipo liked his with sausage. This is his recipe for Chicken Scarpariello. Hope you enjoy it.

SHOEMAKER'S CHICKEN RECIPE

1 whole broiler chicken cut up into 8 pieces
4-6 links of fresh Italian pork sausage, either sweet or hot, or a combination
2 sprigs of rosemary, 8 cloves Garlic
2 red bell peppers cut into ¾ inch slices
Pepperoncino (crushed Red Pepper)
Salt & Black Pepper to taste
Blanche sausage in simmering water for six minutes.

Season chicken with salt and pepper. Place chicken in a large frying pan with olive oil and brown chicken on all sides for about 12 - 15 minutes until nicely browned and crisp. Lower heat to low and let chicken cook on low heat for 10-12 minutes. Turn chicken pieces once.

Remove chicken from pan to a platter. Cut sausage into four pieces each and brown in frying pan. Add peppers and cook with Sausage over medium heat for 7 minutes.

Add chicken back into pan. Cover pan and cook over a low flame for 5 minutes. Take cover off pan, add rosemary and continue cooking for 5 minutes.

Serve each person two to 3 pieces of chicken with sausages and peppers. Serve with a salad, roast or boiled potatoes, or any vegetable you like.

Grandma Bellino's Italian Cookbook

LEMON CHICKEN

Lemon Chicken? This is an Old-School Italian-American recipe that used to be quite popular back in the 50's, 60's, and 70's, but not so popular these days unless you're an Italian-American over 40 years of age. Never the less, making chicken this way is as tasty as ever. Making chicken this way is pure and simple and highlights the good flavors of the chicken. Make some nice Garlic Roasted Potatoes and you're all set with a wonderful refreshing meal. Enjoy.

RECIPE:

1 fresh Broiler Chicken, spit in half
¼ cup Olive Oil
4 cloves Garlic, peeled and sliced thin
2 Lemons, squeezed of their Juice
¼ teaspoon Red Pepper Flakes
¼ teaspoon Sicilian Sea Salt
½ teaspoon Black Pepper
½ cup fresh Parsley, washed and chopped
1 Lemon, sliced thin for garnish

Place chicken in a large bowl with olive oil, Red Pepper, lemon juice, garlic, half the Parsley, and half each of Slat & Black Pepper. Let marinate for at least 3 hours or over night. Mix every hour or two so the chicken gets fully marinated.

Remove from refrigerator and pat dry with paper towels.
Put ¼ cup olive oil in a large oven-proof frying pan that is big enough to fit the 2 chicken halves.

Turn heat to high and put the 2 chicken halves in the pan skin side down. Cook on high heat for 8 minutes.

Turn oven on to 400 degrees.

Turn chicken over to second side and cook on high heat for 7 minutes.

Turn oven down to 375 degrees and cook chicken until done (about 15 minutes).

Serve each person a half or quarter of a chicken, depending on what you prefer.

Serve the chicken with roast or boiled potatoes and or some nice greens like; Escarole, Broccoli Rabe, or Green Beans.

POLLO al MARSALA
Chicken Marsala alla Bellino

This Chicken Marsala has two of Sicily's favorite ingredients, Marsala & Tomatoes. It's super easy to prepare and serves 4 people. To serve up to eight people, just double the recipe.

RECIPE :

1- 3 lb. Chicken
8 tablespoons Olive Oil
Sea Salt & Black Pepper
1 large Onion, peeled and sliced
14 Button Mushrooms, washed and quartered
½ cup Sweet Marsala Wine
1 cup Italian Tomato Passata (crushed Tomato)
1 Bay Leaf
¾ cup water
2 Idaho Potatoes, peeled and cut into large chunks
¼ cup fresh chopped Italian Parsley

Boil the potatoes in boiling salted water for exactly three minutes. Remove from heat and drain in a colander.

Season the chicken pieces with Salt & Black Pepper.

Place Olive Oil in a large frying pan and turn the heat on to high. When the pan and oil are hot, add the chicken pieces to the pan. Cook the chicken until nice and brown on all sides, about 10-12 minutes.

Add mushrooms and cook 5 minutes on high heat. Add onions to pan and cook on medium heat for 6 minutes.

Add Marsala Wine to pan and cook on high heat until the wine is reduce by half its volume, about 5 minutes.

Add tomatoes, potatoes, water, and Bay Leaf to pan and bring to the boil. Once the liquid comes to the boil, low heat, and simmer until the chicken is cooked through, about 25 minutes. Turn heat off.

To serve, plate Chicken, Potatoes, and sauce in even portions on 4 plates. Drizzle with a little Olive Oil and chopped Parsley and serve.

COTOLETTE di POLLO
Chicken Cutlets

In the World of Italian-America, its people and its cuisine, breaded fried Chicken Cutlets are huge, we just love them and eat them all the time. At home we eat them plain, or made into the famed Chicken alla Parmigiano, as part of a *Chicken Sorrentino*, and in a few other guises we eat them too. As concerns my grandmother Giuseppina, it wasn't very often that she'd eat chicken back in Sicily, as Sicilians weren't apt to kill chickens and eat them, but to keep them for their eggs. Once in America however, chickens were greatly more abundant, and cheap to boot. So like most other Italian immigrants to America, my grandmother assimilated to the readily inexpensive and very affordable meat and poultry of America, making Meatballs, Sunday Gravy, and all sorts of Chicken dishes, like; Chicken Cacciatore, Lemon Chicken, as well as these Chicken Cutlets of which my Uncle Tony is especially fond of.

Grandma Bellino's Italian Cookbook

RECIPE:

4 Boneless Chicken Breast (pounded thin)
Salt & Black Pepper, 1 cup flour
1 ½ cups Italian Seasoned Breadcrumbs
2 Large Eggs (beaten)
½ cup Canola, Peanut, or Vegetable Oil for frying

Place the Breadcrumbs, Eggs, and Flour, all in their own separate bowls. Season each with a little Salt & Pepper.

One by one, dredge each Chicken Breast into the flour. Shake off excess flour, then dip into the beaten Eggs. Then place the chicken into the breadcrumbs, pressing crumbs into the chicken, covering the entire surface of each Chicken Breast.

Heat oil in frying pan so it is hot enough that it will immediately start frying the chicken when it's put into the pan, cook all the chicken about 3 minutes on each side, then remove from pan.

Serve the Chicken Cutlets with a nice little mixed green salad, roast potatoes, Green Beans or whatever vegetable you'd like to have with it.

NOTE: You can use Plain Breadcrumbs instead of the Seasoned Italian ones if you like.

To MAKE VEAL PARMIGIANO, make these cutlets, top each with a little Tomato Sauce, grated Parmesan Cheese, and a couple slices of Mozzarella. Bake in the oven at 375 degrees for 6 minutes and serve.

CONIGUGHU alla SALEMI
Nonna's Roast Rabbit alla Salemi

This tasty preparation for Roast Rabbit is from the town of Salemi in Italy. Salemi happens to be my Grandmother Giuseppina's maiden name. This is the simplest and one of the tastiest ways to make rabbit that I know, and that's to roast it with fragrant garlic, Rosemary, onions, with a little touch of white wine. Once you brown the rabbit and vegetables, you can pop the rabbit in the oven to cook. If you're having a dinner party you will double or triple the recipe. As the Rabbit is cooking in the oven, you can serve your guest salad or a pre-made antipasto, and you can sit down and enjoy your guests and antipasto while the rabbit slowly roast in the oven.

RECIPE :

1 young Rabbit, about 2 ¼ pounds
¼ cup Olive Oil
4 tablespoons Flour
¼ cup Dry White Wine
6 cloves Garlic, Peeled and left whole
3 sprigs Fresh Rosemary
Sea Salt & Ground Black Pepper
2 large Baking Potatoes (Idaho)
¼ cup chopped fresh Parsley

Remove four legs from the rabbit. After removing the legs, you will have the center loin and breast flaps left. Cut the flaps off and cut into 4 pieces. You know have the center loin left. Cut this into four pieces. Season all of the rabbit pieces with Salt & Black Pepper. Dredge the rabbit pieces in the flour, and shake off excess.

Place olive oil in a large frying pan and turn heat on. Cook the rabbit over medium heat until all the rabbit is nicely browned, about 10-12 minutes. Remove rabbit from pan and set aside in a bowl.

Leave the olive oil in the pan, add the potatoes and cook on high heat for 5 minutes. Add the onions and cook on low heat for 5 minutes. Add garlic cloves and cook on medium heat for 3 minutes. Remove everything from pan, including the oil and pour over the rabbit in the bowl.

Pour wine into the pan. Turn heat on to high and deglaze the pan by scraping the bottom of the pan with a wooden spoon to dislodge the browned bits sticking to the bottom of the pan. Cook until the wine is reduced by half it original volume.

Add water to pan. Return the rabbit, potatoes, and onions to the pan with all the juices in the bowl. Add Rosemary. Turn heat on and bring to the boil. Cover the pan with a lid or some aluminum foil and bake covered in a 350 degree oven for 30 minutes.

Remove covering from pan and continue baking in the oven for 15 minutes more.

Place potatoes and a few pieces of rabbit on each of 3-4 plates, leaving the juices in pan. Put the pan on a burner on top of the stove and turn heat on high. Cook over high heat to reduce the sauce and make it a bit thicker if it needs it. Turn heat off.

Pour the sauce in equal portions over the rabbit. Sprinkle with chopped Parsley and serve.

CONIGHIU alla SIRACUSANA
Braised Rabbit in The Style of Siracusa

RECIPE :

1 whole Rabbit, cut in 8 pieces by your butcher
1 small Onion, peeled and chopped
2 stalks Celery, chopped
1 Red Bell Pepper, cored and cut in strips
3/4 cup Large Green Olives, pits removed
3 tablespoons Capers from Pantelleria, washed
3 cloves Garlic, peeled
½ cup White Wine, 1 bay leaf
3 tablespoons Red Wine Vinegar
4 whole San Marzano Tomatoes
Sea Salt & Black Pepper
2 large Potatoes, peeled and cut into large cubes
¼ cup fresh chopped Italian Parsley

Place olive oil in a medium frying pan and turn heat on to medium high. Put rabbit in pan, and cook on all sides until the rabbit is nicely browned. Remove rabbit and set aside.

Add Red Bell Peppers to the pan and cook on low heat for 8 minutes. Add onion and celery to pan and cook on medium heat for 4 minutes.

Add garlic to pan and cook on low heat for 2 minutes. Add wine to pan and cook on high heat until the wine reduces by half its volume. About 6-7 minutes.

Add tomatoes to and cook on high heat for 4 minutes. Return the rabbit to the pan and add the vinegar and bay leaf and a half cup water. Add Green Olives and Capers and bring to the boil.

Once all comes to the boil, lower to a simmer and cook on low heat until the rabbit is tender, about 35 minutes or so.

As the rabbit is cooking, cook the potatoes in boiling water for 6 minutes. Remove from water and drain, then put the potatoes in with the rabbit after it has been cooking for about 20 minutes. Let the rabbit and potatoes cook for 15 minutes more. Turn heat off and let set for 10 minutes before serving.

This amount of Rabbit will serve two to three people. If you want to cook for more, double all the ingredients of recipe. When serving, give each person an equal amount of Rabbit and potatoes. Sprinkle with a little Olive Oil and chopped Parsley.

SAUSAGE & BEANS

Another wonderful peasant dish, Sausage & Beans is economical, hearty, and easy to prepare. Sausage fans will especially love it. Anyway, this is a dish my mom always talked about my grandmother making and how much my Uncles Tony, Frank, and Jimmy loved the dish. I know I do, and you will to. It's a dish that takes just a little over a half hour to make and you're ready to eat.

Ingredients:

12 Sweet Italian Sausages
¼ cup Olive Oil
1 medium sized Red Bell Pepper, peeled and chopped
1 large onion, peeled and chopped to medium dice
5 cloves Garlic, peeled and sliced thin
½ teaspoon of crushed Red Pepper Flakes
1 – 14 oz. can Crushed Tomatoes
2 – 14 oz. cans Cannellini Beans, drained & washed
½ teaspoon of Sea Salt & ½ tsp. Black Pepper
1 Bay Leaf
1 cup water
½ cup chopped fresh Parsley (optional)

Prick each piece of sausage with the tip of a sharp knife in a few places each. Put 3 tablespoons of olive oil in a large frying pan with all the sausages and cook on a low flame for 8-10 minutes. Lightly brown the sausages on all sides. Remove from heat and set aside to later.

Place the remaining olive oil in a 6-quart non-corrosive pot with the chopped Red Bell Peppers. Turn flame on to medium and cook for 6 minute. Add onion, low flame to low and cook for 7 minutes. Add garlic and cook 3 minutes, being careful not to let the garlic burn. A red pepper flakes and cook 1 minute.

Add tomatoes, salt, black pepper, and Bay Leaf. Turn heat to high and cook 3 minutes while stirring with a wooden spoon. Add all the sausages. Lower flame to low-medium flame and cook 12 minutes, stirring occasionally.

Add water and beans. And bring liquid up to the boil. Once all comes to the boil. Lower flame, so the liquid is at a low simmer. Let simmer for 10 minutes, and stir occasionally. Turn heat off and let set for 8 minutes before serving.

To serve, fill each persons bowl with the beans and tomato. Top with 3 pieces of sausage each. Sprinkle with chopped parsley on top (if using), and sprinkle top with olive oil.

Grandma Bellino's Italian Cookbook

SALSICCIA e CAVOLFIORE
Cauliflower & Sausage

This hearty dish combines two of our favorite things, Sausage & Cauliflower. It originates from the area around Sicily's famous volcano Mount Etna along with; Taormina, Messina, and Catania too. I highly suggest you try and get yourself a nice bottle of Etna Rosso Wine to drink with your meal.

RECIPE :

6 tablespoons Olive Oil
1 head Cauliflower, 4 Anchovy Filets, minced
1/4 cup large Green Olives, pits removed
1 medium Onion, peeled and chopped
8 Scallions, sliced
½ cup grated Provolone or Caciocavallo Cheese
1 ½ pounds Sweet Fennel Sausage
¼ teaspoon each of Sea Salt & Black Pepper

Remove the core from the cauliflower and discard. Cut cauliflower into florets.

Place olive oil, onions, Anchovies, and half the scallions in a 4-quart pot and cook on medium heat for 5 minutes over medium heat.

Add cauliflower, Green Olives, and Red Wine to pot. Add water to cover the cauliflower. Cook over low heat for 30 minutes.

As the cauliflower is cooking, place the sausages in a large frying pan and cover with water. Cook over low simmering heat for 10 minutes. Remove water from pan and place 3 tablespoons of olive oil in the pan and cook the sausages over low heat, until they are golden brown. Turn heat off when done.

After the cauliflower has been cooking 30 minutes, add most of the remaining scallions to pot with the grated cheese and mix. Cook at low heat, stirring occasionally for 10 minutes. Turn heat off after 10 minutes. The contents should have a little bit of liquid (not much). If too dry, add a bit more water and cook 5 minutes longer.

Turn the heat off and let rest for 5 minutes.

To serve, place some of the Cauliflower on a plate, making a bed for the Sausages. Sprinkle a little olive oil on top along with a little bit of the remaining Scallions to each plate. Top the cauliflower with 3 links of sausage.

NOTE: This is most always served as a main-course dish. But it also makes a nice antipasto, whereby you would use less cauliflower and top with one link of sausage per serving.

Place sausages in a pan and cover with water.

BRASSATO di AGNELLO
Sicilian Braised Lamb Shanks

When making this dish, you are actually making two dishes in one. You are cooking the Lamb Shanks with tomatoes and wine until the lamb is tender. You will be serving the Lamb with the Potatoes, Carrots, and Peas. As you cook the lamb, you are making a sauce for pasta, as well, as this amount of tomatoes is too much for the lamb, but it's there to make some pasta sauce, which you can serve a small plate of before you serve the lamb. Or save the sauce to serve on some pasta the next day. "Yum!" Making this dish is quite a thrifty way to save time, as well as money. That's Italian! And it's Sicilian too! Mangia!

RECIPE :

4 Lamb Shanks
4 Carrots, peeled
2 stalks Celery, washed and cut to small dice
2 medium Onion, peeled and chopped fine
6 cloves garlic, Peeled and chopped fine
¼ teaspoon each: Salt &Black Pepper
1 cup dry Red Wine
2 – 28 ounce can crushed Italian Tomatoes
5 tablespoons Tomato Paste
2 Idaho Potatoes, peeled and cut to large chunks
2 sprigs fresh Rosemary, 2 Bay Leafs
2 cups water
1 – 10 ounce box frozen Peas

Place olive oil in a 6-quart non-corrosive pot. Season lamb with salt & pepper. Place lamb in pot and brown over a medium-high flame until the lamb is browned on all sides, about 12 minutes.

Remove lamb from pot and set aside. Add celery to pot and cook on high heat until light brown, about 8 minutes.

Add onions and cook on medium heat for 5 minutes. Add garlic, lower heat and cook for 2 minutes.

Add the wine and cook on high heat until the wine is reduced by half of its original volume, about 7 minutes.

Add tomatoes, tomato paste, and water to the pot. Add the lamb back to the pot and bring the liquid to boil. As soon as the liquid starts boiling, lower the heat to low and let all simmer for 30 minutes.

Cut the peeled carrots into large chunks.

After the lamb has been cooking for 30 minutes add the Carrots to the pot. Cook 20 minutes more and add the potatoes, rosemary, and Bay Leafs to the pot.

Continue cooking on a low simmer until the lamb is tender, which should be about 25-35 minutes more for a total cooking time of about 1 hour and 20 minutes. Cook the peas in boiling salted water, then drain.

To serve, place one Lamb Shank along with some potatoes, carrots, and peas, and a bit of sauce, saving most of the sauce for pasta the next day.

BISTECCHE PALMERTIANO
Steak al Palermo

This Steak preparation from Palermo is the favorite way that Palermitani like to eat Steak when they are eating it, which is not all that often. Well not all that often 50 years ago or more when most of the population was quite poor. These days however, it's a much different story, people have a little more money these days, and can afford a steak dinner every now and then. Though in the past few years with the world's economy in a downturn, maybe they can't afford steaks all that much once again. This is one reason that the cut of steak is usually cut from the rump or other cheaper cut of beef. In the recipe here however, we have you using Sirloin Steak, though more expensive, it's tastier and more forgiving when cooking it. It will be tender, and not tough as a Rump Steak would be. The dish is almost like a Veal Milanese, a famed Northern Italian dish, Veal Milanese which is quite expensive. Besides it being marinated and that it's beef instead of veal, though similar, the Steak Palmertiano is quite different than it's much more expensive northern cousin.

Being in the Provencia di Palermo in Lercara Friddi, this dish was known to my Sicilian grandfather, who was so poor he only ate it a few times in his life. In America he could have it a bit more often, which was just once a year, cooked by his wife Giuseppina for Philipo's Birthday as a special birthday treat. Make it and treat yourself as well every-now-and-then.

RECIPE :

4 Sirloin Steaks, cut 1/3 of an inch thick
¼ cup Olive Oil, the Juice of 1 Lemon
3 cloves Garlic, peeled and sliced thin
1 bay Leaf
¼ cup chopped fresh Parsley
¼ teaspoon dry Sicilian Oregano
6 tablespoons red wine
1 cup Breadcrumbs
1 Lemon, cut in quarters

Get your butcher to cut you 4 Sirloin Steaks at a thickness of ¾ of an inch each, and have him pound the steaks flat.

Place olive oil, garlic, Lemon Juice, Oregano, wine, and half the fresh Parsley in a shallow glass baking dish and mix all together. Place the steaks in the marinade and let marinate for at least 3 or hours or overnight.

After the steaks have marinated, remove from marinade and shake off excess.

Coat steaks with breadcrumbs on both sides.

Put 8 tablespoons vegetable oil in a large frying pan that is big enough to cook two teaks at a time. Heat oil to high and add two of the steaks. Cook the steaks over medium-high heat for about 3 minutes. Turn steaks over and cook on second side for three minutes.
Remove the two cooked steaks and place in a 200 degree oven on a plate or pan to keep warm.

Cut the other two steaks the same as the first two. When all four steaks are cooked, plate onto 4 plates and sprinkle on the remaining Parsley over the steaks.

Garnish each plate with a lemon wedge and serve steaks with a Mixed Green Salad, Potatoes, or whichever vegetable you like.

Grandma Bellino's Italian Cookbook

POLPETTONE al NONNA
Grandma's Sicilian Meatloaf

This Meatloaf was without question one of my mom's top 10 most popular dishes. She made it often. She got the recipe from her mom, of course. My Mom (Lucia) would make this Meatloaf a couple times a month. If there were any leftovers, mommy would make us tasty Meatloaf Sandwiches for lunch the next day. If you want to double up the recipes and make two Meatloaf's instead of one, making sure of those sandwiches for your lunch the next day or two, it would be a good idea to do so.

RECIPE:

1/2 pound each of ground Beef, Veal, & Pork
1 teaspoon each Sea Salt & Black Pepper
1 medium Onion, peeled and minced
¾ cup fresh Parsley, chopped
2 Eggs, beaten
¼ grated Caciocavallo Cheese
4 tablespoons Golden Currants
4 tablespoons Pignoli Nuts
¼ cup Tomato Sauce
1 cup stale Bread, cut in cubes and soaked in a cup of water
¼ cup of Tomato Ketchup
4 X-Large Eggs, boiled & peeled

Place all the ingredients, except for the Hard Boiled Eggs, 1/3 of the Parsley, Bread & Water, and the Ketchup in a large glass mixing bowl. Mix with your hands until all the ingredients are thoroughly mixed.

Squeeze water out of bread. Break bread into smaller pieces, add to meat and mix with hands.

Line a glass meatloaf pan with 2 tablespoons olive oil.

Add half the meat mixture into the loaf pan and press down lightly.

Cut off the ends of each Hard Boiled Egg and lay them one after the other down the center of the meat in the pan. Press each down lightly.

Place remaining meat-mixture in pan over the eggs and press down.

Cook meatloaf in a 350 degree oven for 40 minutes.

Spread Ketchup over top of meatloaf. Turn oven down to 325 and continue cooking until the meatloaf is done and the meat is cooked through. About 15 minutes more. Remove from the oven and let rest 15 minutes in pan.

Remove meatloaf from pan, and let rest for 10 minutes before cutting and serving.

To serve cut each person 1 thick piece of meatloaf or two thinner ones, and put on a plate with roast potatoes or whatever vegetable you like. Serve the meatloaf as is with remaining chopped Parsley over the top, or with a little tomato sauce over the top of half the meatloaf on a plate. This Meatloaf is Awesome on a Sandwich the next day.

CAVALO REPIENO
Stuffed Cabbage alla Lucia

RECIPE :

1 medium onion, minced
3 cloves of garlic, minced
6 tablespoons chopped parsley
6 tablespoons bread crumbs
2 eggs, Salt & Pepper to taste
1 cup long grain rice, cooked
1 1/2 pounds Ground Beef
½ cup grated Pecorino Romano
1 medium Head Savoy Cabbage, about 2 lbs.
½ cup chicken broth
½ stick of Butter
¼ cup Olive Oil
2 cups tomato sauce

Cook rice according to directions on package, then let cool. You will end up with 2 cups rice.

Bring a large pot of salted water to the boil. Cut the bottom off of the cabbage. Cut the core out of the cabbage. Cook the cabbage in boiling water for 4-5 minutes, until the cabbage leaves are tender, yet still slightly firm. Drain cabbage and let cool.

In a large mixing bowl, add cooled the rice, onion, garlic, parsley, ground beef, and breadcrumbs.

Season the beef liberally with salt and pepper. Mix with hands.

Add cheese, a ½ cup of the tomato sauce, and eggs, and mix thoroughly.

Take a small handful of the meat mixture and fill each cabbage leave. Place a small amount of the meat mixture about 3 inches from the end of a cabbage leave. Fold the end over the meat. Fold sides in, and then roll cabbage leave up to close. Roll the cabbage leaves until all the meat mixture is gone.

Heat oven to 400 degrees. Coat a shallow glass or ceramic baking pan with the olive oil. Place half of the remaining tomato sauce into pan. Place all the rolled cabbages neatly into pan. Cover with remaining tomato sauce. Add chicken Broth and dot with butter on top.

Cook in oven at 400 degrees for 12 minutes. Lower heat to 350 and continue cooking for about 30 minutes until the meat inside the cabbage is fully cooked.

Take out of oven and let rest for 10 minutes before serving. Serve each person 3 or 4 Stuffed Cabbages with a little sauce. You may serve with roast, boiled, or mashed potatoes or whatever you like.

STUFATO di MANZO
Beef Stew alla Nonna

Beef Stew, who doesn't love it? It's American as Apple Pie. Well, we're talking about Sicilian food here, aren't we? Yes we are. But Sicilians, and most Italians for that matter, love some sort of Beef Stew too. And many Italian immigrants in the first half of the 20th Century would make Beef Stew regularly. This is how my mother made hers from the recipe of here mom, Nonna Giuseppina

RECIPE :

3 pound Beef Chuck, cut into 2" cubes
¼ cup Olive Oil
1 medium Onion, peeled and diced
10 ounces Button Mushrooms, sliced thick
½ cup dry Red Wine
4 Garlic cloves, peeled and sliced
4 Carrots, peeled and cut into large dice
1 cup San Marzano Tomatoes
2 tablespoons Tomato Paste
1 Beef Bullion Cube (optional)
2 Bay Leaves
2 Baking Potatoes, peeled an cut in large dice
2 sprigs fresh Rosemary
½ teaspoon each Sea Salt & Black Pepper
½ lb. package wide Egg Noodles
¼ cup chopped fresh Parsley

Place half the olive oil in a 6-quart pot and cook mushrooms over medium until lightly browned. Add onions and cook for 4 minutes on low heat. Add ¼ teaspoon each of slat & black pepper and cook 1 minute more. Remove from pot and set aside.

Place remaining olive oil in the pot and turn heat on to high. Brown the beef in 3 separate batches over medium to high heat until all the beef is nicely browned.

Set the beef aside when all the pieces are browned. Add 3 tablespoons of flour to pan and cook on low heat in the oil and pan drippings from the beef, while stirring with a wooden spoon. Cook 4-5 minutes.

Add wine and turn heat on to high and let cook until the wine reduces by half, about 4-5 minutes.

Add 1 ½ cups of water a little at a time while stirring to mix flour and water together, cooking over a medium flame for 3 minutes.

Add beef back top pot and sprinkle the beef with a little salt and pepper.

Add tomatoes, tomato paste, carrots, garlic, and bay leaf. Put the mushrooms & onions back in the pot and cook on high heat for 5 minutes.

Add water to just barely cover the meat. Add bullion cube. Bring to the boil. Once all comes to the boil, lower to a steady simmer and let cook for 1 hour and ten minutes.

Add potatoes to pot and continue cooking until the beef is nice and tender. About 25 minutes more. Turn heat off.

Cook the egg noodles according to directions on package. When done cooking drain in a colander.
Put the noodles back in the pot they cooked in and add the butter. Mix.

Place some noodles on each plate for your guest, then top with a good portion of the stew for each plate. Drizzle with a little olive oil and sprinkle a little chopped parsley on each plate and serve.

VITELLO MARSALA al ANTONIO
Veal Marsala Uncle Tony's Way

Not your typical Veal Marsala that you'd see in many an Italian Restaurants around the country. Mostly all restaurants make Veal Marsala with the cut of meat called Scaloppini. This version my Uncle Tony makes, is by far *the best Veal Marsala* I've ever had anywhere. He makes his with veal shoulder instead of the scaloppini you usually see. This is the old-school Sicilian way. The way he learned from watching his mother make it, after he'd bring home a nice piece of Veal that he got from the butcher shop he worked at, Scarlotta's in Lodi. Using the veal shoulder makes this a stew rather than a scaloppini dish, which must be eaten right away once cooked. With the stew you can make it ahead, refrigerate it, then re-heat it when you're going to serve it, making this a great dish for entertaining guests for a dinner party

PS .. Veal Marsala made with Scallopini has been pretty popular in the U.S. for many years. Marsala is the famous Sweet wine from the western Sicilian city of Marsala, the Marsala being, along with the veal, the main components of the dish.

RECIPE: UNCLE TONY'S VEAL MARSALA

1 ½ pounds Veal Shoulder, cut in 2" square pieces
1 small onion, peeled and diced fine
6 ounces Button Mushrooms
2 ounces Dry Porcini Mushrooms, reconstituted
½ cup good quality Sweet Marsala Wine
1 tablespoon Butter, 2 tablespoons Olive Oil
1 tablespoon flour
¼ cup chopped fresh Italian Parsley (not dried)

Heat a large frying pan that is large enough to hold all the veal. Add olive oil. Pat all the veal dry with a paper towel. Season the veal with salt & Black Pepper. Add veal to pan. Brown over high heat until all the veal is nicely browned.

Add ¾ of the Marsala Wine and let reduce to half its original volume. Once you add the wine, scrape the bottom of pan with a wooden spoon. This loosens the brown bits that stick to bottom of the pan. These brown bits are full of flavor and are key in making a good sauce.

Once the Marsala has reduced by half, remove the Veal and the cooking juice from pan and set aside.

Add 2 tablespoons olive oil and 1 of butter to the pan. Add fresh mushrooms and cook over Medium heat until mushrooms are cooked through. About 6-7 minutes. Remove from Pan and set aside.

Add 2 tablespoons of butter to pan. Add veal back to pan without juices. Turn heat on low and cook for 1 minute. Sprinkle flour evenly over veal while stirring. Cook at low heat for 2 minutes. Add remaining Marsala Wine and Cook at low heat 2 minutes.

Add veal juices to pan. Add Porcini Mushrooms. Add 1 cup chicken stock. Simmer Veal for 1 hour and 15 minutes over very low heat.

Add fresh mushrooms to pan, cook for 15 minutes more. Veal should be nice and tender. Serve Veal Marsala with boiled or mashed Potatoes. Serve each person and sprinkle fresh chopped Parsley over top.

COSTELETTE di MAILE
Pork Chops Italian Style

RECIPE :

8 Center Cut Pork Chops
3 Red Bell Peppers, washed and cored
1 medium Onion, peeled and sliced thick
1/2 cup Olive Oil, Sea Salt & ground Black Pepper
3 Idaho Potatoes, peeled
¼ cup chopped fresh Parsley (optional)

Wash the Red Peppers, cut in half and remove core from peppers. Cut each half into 4 strips lengthwise.

Place in a small glass or ceramic baking dish with 1/3 of the Olive Oil. Cook in a 325-degree oven for 25 minutes.

While the peppers are roasting, start the potatoes. Cut each potato in half lengthwise, then cut each of these half in-half again down the length. You now have 4 long pieces. Cut each one of these in 5 pieces. Put the potatoes in a large frying pan with olive oil and cook on high heat for 6 minutes, getting the potatoes a bit brown.

Season potatoes with salt & pepper and continue cooking over low heat for 10 minutes. Add onions to the pan and cook on low heat for 7 minutes. Turn off heat and put in the pan with Roast Red Peppers after they have been cooking for 25 minutes. Continue cooking at 325 degree for 15 minutes.

Season the pork chops with Salt & Black Pepper on each side. Heat a large frying pan to high and add remaining Olive Oil. Cook the pork chops in two batches. Place 4 pork chops in a pan and cook on high heat, getting pork chops nicely browned. Cook for 5-6 minutes on the first side. Turn pork chops over and cook on 2nd side for 3 minutes on high heat.

Turn oven down to 200 degrees. Place the 4 cooked pork chops in the pan with the peppers to keep warm while you cook the remaining 4 Pork Chops.

Cook the remaining 4 Pork Chops the same way you did the first four, 5-6 minute on high heat on first side. Turn Pork Chops over to 2nd side and cook 3 minutes on high heat.

Place two Pork Chops on each of 4 plates, to one side of the plate. Top each pork chop with some of the Peppers & Onions. Place equal amounts of Roast Potatoes on each plate, pour any juices in pan over each plate of pork chops. Sprinkle each plate with chopped Parsley and serve.

SPEZZATINO di VITELLO
Italian Veal Stew

INGREDIENTS:

2 ½ pounds Veal Stewing Meat
5 tablespoons olive oil, 1 tablespoon Butter
Salt & Black Pepper
1 medium Onion, peeled and diced
1 pound Button Mushrooms, quartered
2 stalks Celery, diced
2 Carrots, peeled and sliced
½ cup Dry White Wine
3 cups water
3 tablespoons Tomato Paste
1 Bay Leaf
3 tablespoon Cornstarch mixed w/ 6 Tbs. water
3 Idaho Potatoes, peeled & cut into 8 large pieces
10 ounce package Frozen Peas

Cut the Veal into 1 ½ inch cubes.

Place olive oil in a 6-quart no-corrosive pot. Turn heat on to medium pot. Brown the veal on a medium high flame in 2 or 3 batches. Season the veal with salt & pepper as you're browning. Turn veal every few minutes so all side get nicely brown.

Set veal aside when all of it has been browned. Add onions to pan and cook on medium heat for 4-5 minutes. Add wine and cook until the wine is reduced by half, making sure to scrape the bottom of the put with a wooden spoon to dislodge the brown bits on the bottom (these bits are full of flavor and help make the sauce tasty). Remove onion wine mixture from pot and set aside.

Add butter and button mushrooms to pot. Season with salt & pepper. Cook over medium heat for about 7 minutes until the mushrooms are nicely browned. Remove from pot and set aside.

Add the veal, onions, carrots, bay leaf, tomato paste, water. Bring all to the boil. Once this has all come to the boil, low flame so the stew is simmering at a low simmer. Cook 1 hour and 15 minutes. Mixing occasionally so stew does not stick and burn.

Add the Cornstarch & Water mixture, mix and cook two minutes.

Add potatoes to pot and continue cooking for 35 minutes.

When the stew is almost finished, add the peas and cook for two minutes. The Stew is ready to serve, so dish a plate to everyone and enjoy.

Grandma Bellino's Italian Cookbook

VERDURE

Vegetables? We just love them! We, being Italian-Americans I'm talking about here. We love all kinds of vegetables, like; potatoes, eggplant, mushrooms, peppers, and tomatoes, we are particularly fond of our vegetables that are more or less just Italian, the vegetables that Americans of other ethnic origins have not really discovered until the past 15 years or so. Many still have not. These vegetables that I'm talking about, are our beloved; Escarole (Scarola), Rapini (Broccoli Rabe), and Cucuzza (aka Gagootz). We are Italian, and we love sharing our food, but that being said, we do like keeping a few things to ourselves every-now-and-then. Our little secrets shall we say? Well not secrets completely, but we're not going to broadcast certain things. Well, many Americans have caught on to Broccoli Rabe in recent years, some, but not many to Escarole, and we still have one, that is still almost completely ours, and that's our *Gagootz,* real name Cucuzza. Yes not many other Americans have caught on to this, one of our most beloved Italian vegetables of all, and a veg that is so very Sicilian at that. We make the Gagootz into vegetable side-dishes, into Pasta, and Soups.

Another thing many non-Italian Americans might not know, is that true Italian Cuisine is based more on vegetables than any other cuisine in the World. Yeah, I know, you thought it was pasta. Well yes, and no. And as far as pasta and vegetables go, the most popular Italian dish of all, if you omit the grated cheese, it's all vegetable. What is it you ask?

Spaghetti with Tomato Sauce (Spaghetti Pomodoro) of course! The Sugo di Pomodoro is all vegetable; tomatoes, olive oil, and garlic. And pasta? Technically, the wheat is in the vegetable family.

Yes, we love our vegetables; we have them as side-dishes (contorni), for antipasti as with; Caponata, and Stuffed Mushrooms or Roast Peppers, and in many pasta other dishes, or as a main course with our most prized veg dish, Eggplant Parmigiano.

Vegetables are vital to the Italian diet. Make sure you get 5-6 servings of fruits and vegetables every day, they will help you stay healthy. It's true, "you are what you eat," and if you eat a lot of junk, your body will turn to junk. I don't want to get too philosophical, but it's true.

So, eat your vegetables, try some new ones, like Cucuzza or Scarola if you've never had them before. Try them, cook them, eat healthy and enjoy. Here are a few popular vegetable dishes for you to try below.

FRITTEDDI
Melange of Vegetables Sicilian Style

INGREDIENTS :

1/2 cup Olive Oil
8 Scallions, washed and sliced
6 cloves Garlic, left whole
10 ounces frozen Fava Beans, defrosted
6 frozen Artichoke Bottoms, defrosted & sliced
1 – 10 box frozen Peas, thawed
½ pound fresh Green Beans, ends removed
¾ teaspoon each of Sea Salt & Black Pepper

Cook the Green Beans in boiling salted water for 4 minutes. Drain in a colander and run cold water over beans to stop cooking. Shake off excess water.

Place olive oil in a large pot with garlic and cook for two minutes on medium heat. Add green beans, turn heat to high and cook. Add Artichokes and cook 4 minutes on medium heat.

Add Scallions to pot and cook on low heat for 7 minutes.

Add Fava Beans and cook for 3 minutes on medium heat while stirring. Add Salt & Black Pepper and mix.

Add Peas and cook on medium heat for 4 minutes.

This wonderful medley of mixed vegetables is most often eaten as a side dish (Contorni) for any fish, meat, or poultry dishes. It's also great as an antipasto on its own or part of a antipasti misti (Mixed Antipasto).

For a great lunch or brunch, Fry or Scramble two eggs and serve these mixed vegetables along with the eggs.

SCAROLA
SAUTÉED ESCAROLE

Escarole (Scarola) is by far the favorite vegetable of Italian-America, we just love it. We stuff it, it's in a couple of our favorite soups, like Escarole & Bean and Italian Wedding Soup, and here, the way we eat it most, sautéed in olive oil with garlic, to go on the side of our chicken, fish, or meat course, or as a nice simply antipasto to start a great meal. E' Scarola!

Ingredients:

2 heads escarole washed and roughly chopped
7 cloves garlic, peeled and sliced
¼ teaspoon crushed red pepper
Sea Salt (to taste)
¼ cup olive oil

Sauté garlic in oil until it just begins to brown. Add red pepper, to oil and cook 1 minute.

Shake most of the water off the escarole, but let some still cling on, it will help it to cook.

Add Escarole and sauté over medium heat for about 6 minutes.

Cook the escarole in 2 – 3 batches in a large skillet pan. Season with Salt & Black Pepper and serve.

RAPINI
Sautéed Broccoli Rabe

We Italians have been eating Broccoli Rabe all our lives. Lately, many Americans not of Italian ancestry have discovered the wonders of this nutritious vegetable that we've been enjoying for quite a while now. Broccoli Rabe is packed with Potassium, Iron, dietary fiber, and has Vitamins A, C, & K. This vegetable also contains Lutein which is strong Antioxidant that protects the retinas in our eyes. Broccoli Rabe is a Super Food that is one of the most nutrient dense foods on the Planet, and it taste good too. What more could you want?

PREPARATION :

1 pound bunch of fresh Broccoli Rabe (Andy Boy)
2-3 cloves Garlic, peeled and coarsely chopped
7 tablespoons Italian Olive Oil
a pinch of Pepperoncino (Red Pepper Flakes)
Sea Salt & Black Pepper

Cut ends of Broccoli Rabe and any blemishes if there are any. Wash in cold running water. Cut Broccoli Rabe in to 2 or 3 pieces for each stem.

Bring a pot of water to the boil, and add one tablespoon salt.

Cook the Broccoli Rabe in rapidly boiling water for 3 minutes. Drain, and put the Broccoli Rabe under cold running water for 2 minutes. Drain.

Heat a large frying pan over medium heat. Add Olive Oil and Garlic. Cook garlic over medium heat 2 to 3 minutes until the garlic starts to get a little brown on the edges. Lower heat to very low, add Red Pepper. Cook 1 minute over low heat. Add the drained Broccoli Rabe and turn heat up to high. Cook over high heat for about 5 minutes, and serve immediately.

Note: As stated earlier, you can make a wonderful antipasto of this cooked Broccoli Rabe topped with 1 piece of cooked Italian Sweet or Hot Sausage on top. Serve 3 pieces with the Broccoli Rabe for a main course. Another wonderful item is a Rapini & Salsiccia Bruschetta. Break up 2 or 3 pieces of Italian Sweet or Hot Sausage and cook. Cut the Broccoli Rabe to smaller pieces and cook as in the above recipe. Add Sausage to Broccoli Rabe. Cut Italian or French Bread into half inch slices and toast. Rub the toasted bread with a pieced of raw garlic (great flavor). Top each piece of toasted bread with some of the Sausage and Broccoli Rabe mixture and serve. Your guest will love it. And they'll love you too. Bravo! See all you can do with Broccoli Rabe? You had know idea, did you? Enjoy!

ZUCCHINI e POMDORINI

1 medium Onion, peeled and sliced
¼ cup Olive Oil
4 medium Zucchini, scrubbed & washed
3 cloves Garlic, peeled and sliced
¼ teaspoon Pepperoncino (Red Pepper)
¼ teaspoon each of Salt & Black Pepper
1 ½ cups Cherry Tomatoes, washed

Cut each Zucchini down the center lengthwise. Then cut the zucchini into sliced.

Add olive oil and onions to a 3-quart pot and cook on medium heat for 4 minutes.

Add zucchini and cook on high heat for 6 minutes, stirring occasionally. Add garlic and red pepper flakes and cook on low heat for 2 minutes.

Add Salt & Black Pepper and mix.

Add Cherry Tomatoes and cook on high heat for 3 minutes.

Lower heat to low and cook for 12 minutes on low heat.

Serve as a vegetable side dish (Contorni), as an antipasto, or for a nice lite lunch, scramble or fry 2 eggs and serve with the zucchini, e Mangia Bene.

PATATE ARROSTO
Roast Potatoes

Roasting Potatoes in this manner is popular all over Italy, especially in Tuscany and with Sicilians. They are the perfect accompaniment for just about any grilled or roast Fish, Meat, or Poultry, and along with a Frittata or Fried Eggs for breakfast or light lunch. These potatoes are extremely versatile and should be in every good cooks repertoire. Put them in yours.

5 Idaho Baking Potatoes
¼ cup Olive Oil
¼ teaspoon each of Sea Salt & Black Pepper
3 sprigs fresh Rosemary
5 clove of Garlic, peeled and left whole

Wash the potatoes and cut in half long-ways. Then cut each half-potato in-half length-ways again, then cut each of these long strips into 5 pieces each. Cut each potato this way (you want cubes 1 /2 to 2" each).

Place all the ingredients except the garlic in a glass or ceramic baking dish and mix with a spoon.

Place in a 350 degree oven and bake for 20 minutes.

Add the garlic to the potatoes and mix. Cook for 15 minutes more. Take out of oven, and let set for five minutes before serving.

CANNAZZO
Roast Vegetables Sicilian Style

INGREDIENTS :

4 small or 4 medium sized Eggplants
4 medium sized Zucchini
1 Yellow Bell Pepper and 1 Red Bell Pepper
1 large Onion, peeled and cut to large dice
2 large Baking Potatoes (Idaho) peeled
6 cloves Garlic, peeled and left whole
¼ cup Olive Oil
4 Anchovy filets (optional)
Sea Salt & Black Pepper
¼ cup chopped fresh Italian Parsley

Wash Zucchini & Eggplants and cut to 1 1/2 inch cubes (leave skin on) and add to a large glass or ceramic baking pan. Add onions, garlic, & Olive Oil.

Cut bell peppers in half and remove core, seed, & stem. Cut into 1 ½ " pieces and add to baking pan. Peel potatoes and cut into 1" cubes, and add to pan.

Mix all the vegetables together, coating completely with Olive Oil. Add Sea Salt & Black Pepper to taste and mix all vegetables together again.

Place pan with vegetables in a 350 degree oven and cook for 45 minutes, stirring the vegetables every 15 minutes until done. Remove from oven and serve as a side dish or antipasto. Sprinkle with fresh Parsley. Can be served as a Main Course for Vegetarians.

PANINI
Italian-American Sandwiches

We Italians do love our sandwiches, Italians in both Italy and here in America, and we have some of the World's greatest. Greatest Sandwiches that is! Of course there are Sausage & Peppers, Meatball Parms, la Vasteddi, Pepper & Eggs, and the Submarine, a.k.a. Sub Sandwich, or just simply *Subs*, which are Hoagies in South Jersey & Philadelphia, with *Grinders* up in there in New England. Sub Sandwiches can be made with a multitude of different ingredients, but the most popular is with Salami, Ham, and Provolone, that are dressed with thinly sliced raw onion, Tomato, Olive Oil, Lettuce, Vinegar, Oregano, with Salt & Pepper sprinkled on top. If you like, the Italian Deli or Pizzeria that you're at will top it with some Hot Cherry Peppers as well.

Yes, the Sub is quite popular, but have you ever heard of Italian Beef from Chicago or the super tasty Muffuletta Sandwich from the Central Grocery in New Orleans, home of one of the largest Sicilian American populations in the whole country? Most of you have probably not heard of either unless you live in or have been to these two famous American Cities, both with large Italian populations. You may have not heard of Italian Beef or the Muffuletta, but everyone, no matter where they live in the United States has heard and know of that famous sandwich from The City of Brotherly Love, Philadelphia, PA.

But although, most Americans have heard, know of, and have probably eaten a Philly Cheese Steak at some point in their lives, very few know that the sandwich (originally No Cheese) was invented by an Italian-American. Yes, it's a sandwich of Philadelphia, never-the-less it was invented by a Philadelphian of Italian ancestry, making it Italian.

Well "that Muffuletta," you say, what is it? Well it's very similar to a Sub Sandwich, it's stuffed with Ham, Salami, Mortadella, and Provolone, but the difference is the bread, which is called *Muffoletta* and is a large round-loaf, and is where the sandwich gets its name. The spelling of the sandwich is the Muffuletta, dropping the "o" in Muffoletta for another "u," and the sandwich is Muffuletta. So, the bread is a bit different, but the biggest difference and what really makes it a Muffuletta is the tasty and chunky Olive Salad, made up of Big Green Sicilian Olives, Roast Red Pepper, Cauliflower, Olive Oil, Salt, Pepper, and Vinegar. This salad is chopped and tops the cheese and meats inside the Muffoletta Bread, and Voila, you've got a *Muffuletta*, one of the World's Great Sandwiches, and more or less only to be found in the great city of New Orleans and its environs. If you've never had one of these babies, you gotta go down there and get yourself one, they're awesome!

So, yes we love our sandwiches in the Italian-American enclave, and we've invented a few famous ones at that, sandwiches that sell millions every year. But when it comes to making them at home we have a few that are a bit different, and some *secret*. These sandwiches are more or less made at home and just in a few Italian Delis *here and there*. And these sort of *secret sandwiches* are mostly made with eggs. What are they you say? Well there is the very popular Pepper & Egg Sandwich (*Pep & Egg*) that's made all year round, but especially popular during the Lenten Season when Catholics don't eat meat at all, or at least not on Fridays, so they might have one of these sandwiches for Friday lunch, and fish at dinner-time. These same Pepper Eggs get a nice addition once Lent is over, in the form of Italian Sweet or Hot Sausages and a Sausage Pepper & Egg Sandwich. Often we'll stuff a sandwich with a Frittata that was made earlier in the day or the day before. And some families have their own special Italian inspired sandwiches like our family does in the form of my Aunt Helen's famous Spinach and Egg Sandwich that we call *The Aunt Helen Special*. It's an awesome sandwich, and my friends who I've made it for, go absolutely bonkers for it, and always ask me to make it.

Sausage & Peppers is after The Sub, one of the most famous and most widely eaten Italian-American Sandwiches of all. We love eating them at Italian Festivals, from the local Pork Store or Pizzeria, and we make them quite often at home, especially when we are having a barbecue, they're the perfect little treat. And when we make Spaghetti & Meatballs or the famed Sunday Gravy on Sunday, we always make extra Meatballs, so we can make ourselves a tasty Meatball Parm Sandwich the next day. When it comes to sandwiches, we do love them quite a bit. Sandwiches are second only to pasta in the Italian-American community, and we just love them!

PEP & EGGS *"The Original"*

This is the classic Italian-American *Pepper & Eggs Sandwich* (Pep & Egg) that's quite popular in Italian neighborhoods in and around Chicago and in the southern New England states, especially in Rhode Island, Connecticut, and the Boston Metro area. It's a simple tasty sandwich that's quick and easy to make.

INGREDIENTS:

¼ cup Olive Oil
1 each Red & Green Bell Pepper, wash and remove core and stems and sliced to ¼" strips
1 medium Onion, peeled and sliced
2 cloves Garlic, peeled and sliced
Salt & Ground Black Pepper
6 Extra Large Eggs
1 loaf Crusty Italian Bread or 4 Hard Rolls

Place olive oil and all the Peppers in a large frying pan and cook on medium heat for 4 minutes. Lower flame to low and cook for 10 minutes, stirring occasionally.

Add onions and cook on low heat for 8 minutes. Add garlic and cook on low heat for 3 minutes.

Turn the heat up to high and add the eggs. Cook over high heat while stirring for a minute and a half. Lower heat and finish cooking, about 3 minutes.

Cut the loaf of bread in half, lengthwise and fill with Peppers & Eggs. Cut into four equal pieces and serve.

PEPPER & EGGS
alla SICILIANO-AMERICANO

This is the Pepper & Eggs that we of Sicilian ancestry like to make. It's made the same as the standard Pepper & Eggs which is quite awesome in and of itself. But we being Sicilian and loving our favorite cheese Caciocavallo, we like to grate some and add it to the normal Pepper and Eggs, along with some lightly fried potatoes. This sandwich is supremely tasty, we're sure you'll agree.

To make Pepper & Eggs alla Siciliano, cut 2 medium sized baking potatoes into small cubes and sauté in olive oil until golden brown. Season the potatoes with salt and black pepper.

Follow the Pepper & Eggs recipe above, add these sautéed potatoes to the pepper & onion after they are finished cooking. Add ¼ cup of chopped parsley and cook the peppers, onions, & potatoes for 1 minute. Add the eggs and cook until done.

Cut a loaf of Italian Bread or Rolls down the middle, add the Pepper & Eggs and top the eggs with some grated Caciocavallo. Cover with top piece of bread and serve.

Grandma Bellino's Italian Cookbook

THE AUNT HELEN SPECIAL

The Aunt Helen Special? I wasn't going to include this recipe in this book, but since I mentioned it in the intro to this chapter, I figured it would be a tease and just not right to mention it and then not include a recipe for how to make it. So her it is. You're not going to believe how amazingly delicious this simple little sandwich is when made correctly. Try it, and I'm sure you will agree.

INGREDIENTS:

2 small Italian Hero Rolls or Any Roll You Like
4 large Eggs
Salt & Black Pepper
1 ½ cups chopped cooked Spinach (fresh or frozen)
½ cup grated Parmigiano Reggiano or Grana Padano
2 tablespoons Olive Oil, 1 tablespoon Butter

Beat eggs with Salt & Pepper to taste.

Sauté spinach for 3-4 minute low heat. Season with Salt & Pepper.

Place eggs in a bowl. Add grated cheese, Salt & Pepper, and beat eggs with a fork.

Turn heat up to high. Add eggs and cook over high heat while constantly stirring eggs with a wooden spoon or rubber spatula until the eggs are cooked completely. Remove eggs from pan and leave on the side.

Add a tiny bit each of olive oil and butter to pan and toast the rolls in the pan until all four halves rolls are lightly toasted.

Place the 2 bottoms of the rolls on plates, divide the scrambled eggs and spinach in to 2 equal parts and place on each bottom half of toasted rolls. If you like at this point you can sprinkle a bit of Salt & pepper over the eggs then top with a bit more Parmigiano. Top with top of roll, cut each sandwich in half, and enjoy. You your friends will love this one.

Note: As stated before, you can serve these eggs on toasted Crostini Bread at a cocktail hour or as the Antipasto or part of Antipasto Misto for the first course of a meal. You can also serve the Uovo Strapazetti (Scrambled Eggs) on a plate by themselves, with a Salad or some other vegetable on the side. Whatever you do, you will be surprised how much flavor and how tasty this simple, versatile dish is. Buon Appetito!

SAUSAGE & PEPPERS
The SANDWICH

It's probably a toss-up which of the Italian-American Sandwiches is Italian-America's favorite. The toss-up is between the much-loved Meatball Parm and this one, Sausage & Peppers. Which is more preferred depends on who you're asking. If you ask an Italian in Philadelphia, he's gonna tell you his favorite sandwich is the Philly Cheese Steak *of course.* But some in Philly may prefer Roast Pork with Broccoli Rabe & Provolone. If you're in Chicago and ask a Windy City Italian, he'll tell you it's Italian Beef, whereby in New Orleans you know it's gonna be a Muffuletta. But when it comes to the country on the whole, the top two Italian Sandwiches are the Meatball Parm or this Sausage & Peppers. What's yours?

How to Make It :

2 Red Bell Peppers
3 medium Onions, peeled and sliced
¼ cup Olive Oil
Salt & Black Pepper
10 Italian Sweet Sausages

Cut the peppers in half, remove the inner core and discard. Cut the peppers in ¼ inch strips and place in a small roasting pan. Season with Salt & Black Pepper and mix. Put Peppers in a 350 degree oven.

In the meantime, start browning the sausages in a frying pan over medium heat. Cook sausages on all side until golden brown, but not too brown. This should take about 10-12 minutes. Turn heat off.

After the Peppers have been roasting in the oven, add the onions and cook for 15 minutes.

Add sausage to pan with the Peppers & Onions and cook at 375 degrees for 5 minutes. Remove peppers & onions from oven and set aside.

Split rolls in half lengthwise and toast. Remove the sausages from the pan and cut each sausage link in-half lengthwise. You should have 20 pieces of Sausage.

Place the 4 bottom pieces down on a work surface. Place 5 pieces of Sausage over each bottom-half roll. Top each with Peppers & Onions. Top each sandwich with the top of the roll each. Cut sandwiches in half and serve to 3 luck guests and yourself.

FRITTATA al PALERMINTANA
Frittata in The Style of Palermo

Frittata have been quite popular among Sicilian Americans since the first days of the great migration to the shores of America around 1900. They are cheap and easy to make, and they make a nice little meal along with a salad. Or you can eat a wedge as a snack anytime of the day at all. They are great to pack in a lunch box when you go to work, for a picnic, or a snack in the car during a long road trip. There are many different ways to make them with many different fillings, such as; Sausage & Peppers, with Mushrooms, with Spaghetti Tomatoes & Cheese or any-way you like, a frittata is always a good thing to have.

RECIPE :

8 Extra Large Eggs
3 tablespoons Olive Oil
8 tablespoons grated Caciocavallo Cheese
2 tablespoons Butter
¼ teaspoon each of Salt & White Pepper
¼ cup Chopped Parsley

You'll need a 10-inch non-stick frying pan that has a heat proof handle so it can go in the oven. Heat oven to 350 degrees.

Crack eggs in a large mixing bowl. Add salt & pepper and beat eggs until they are well mixed.

Add the grated cheese and parsley to eggs and mix.

Set the frying pan on stove-top, add olive oil and butter and turn heat to medium flame. When the butter starts to foam, add the eggs and mix rapidly with a wooden spoon or rubber spatula until eggs tart to set but are still runny on the top, about 3 minutes. Make sure the eggs stay in one whole piece that takes the shape of the pan.

Put the pan in the oven and let the frittata bake for 5 minutes. Remove from oven.

Remove the frittata from the pan and onto a 12" plate all in one piece.
Cut into wedges and eat as a main course with a little salad on the side, or as a antipasto on its own or as part of a mixed antipasto.

You can also serve as a sandwich on a roll on its own or with sliced tomato and or a couple slices of any cheese you like.

FRITTATA alla NONNA
Nonna's Potato & Pancetta Frittata

RECIPE :

2 Idaho Potatoes, peeled
1 medium Onion, peeled and sliced thin
3 ounce Pancetta, diced
10 tablespoons Olive Oil
8 Extra Large Eggs
3 tablespoons Olive Oil
¼ cup grated Caciocavallo Cheese
2 tablespoons Butter
¼ teaspoon each of Sea Salt & White Pepper
¼ cup Chopped Parsley

Cut potatoes in half long-ways. Cut each half into slices slightly thicker than 1/8" …

Cook the potatoes in boiling salted water for exactly 3 minutes. Remove from heat and drain in a colander. Set aside.

You'll need a 10 inch non-stick frying pan that has a heat proof handle so it can go in the oven. Heat oven to 350 degrees. Cook the Pancetta in the pan on low heat for 6 minutes. Remove pancetta from pan and set aside.

Add the Olive Oil and potatoes to pan and cook potatoes on medium heat until they get nicely browned, about 9 minutes.

Add onions and cook on low heat for 6 minutes while stirring with a wooden spoon. Add butter, season potatoes & onions with Salt & Pepper and Pancetta to pan and cook on low heat for 2 minutes.

Crack eggs in a large mixing bowl. Add Sea Salt & Pepper and beat eggs until they are well mixed.

Add the grated cheese and parsley to eggs and mix.

Turn heat to high and add eggs to pan and cook while stirring the eggs for 1-2 minutes.

Place pan in oven to finish cooking the frittata, about 8 minutes.

Remove from oven and let rest five minutes before serving.

NOTE : Serve a smaller wedge of Frittata on its own as an antipasto or a larger wedge with a salad. Serve the frittata at room temperature, warm, or hot from the pan. Save any remaining frittata in the refrigerator to eat cold or heated up for a nice little snack any time of the day.

AUNT FRANS RICOTTA COOKIES

I remember the first time my Aunt Fran made these Ricotta Cookies and served them to us after dinner, I went absolutely crazy. These cookies were so good, I couldn't stop eating them. I know I ate more of those cookies than anyone at the table. I was expecting someone to say something about how I was hogging up the cookies, but no one did, and I kept going for them. I couldn't help myself. After that, every time we'd go to Uncle Tony and Aunt Fran's house for dinner, I was always hoping she made some of the Ricotta Cookies, which she did many times, but not always. Never-the-less we always had more than enough goodies for dessert, but I yearned for Aunt Fran's tasty Ricotta Cookies anyway. I still do to this day. Here is Aunt Fran's awesome recipe for Ricotta Cookies. You're gonna love them!

RECIPE :

1 stick unsalted Butter (at room temperature)
2 cups Granulated Sugar
1 pound Whole Milk Ricotta
½ teaspoon Salt
2 Large Eggs, the Zest of One Orange
1 teaspoon Vanilla Extract
2 ½ cups All Purpose Flour
2 tablespoons Baking Soda
1 ½ tablespoons Baking Powder
¼ cup Powdered 10X Sugar

Cream the butter and sugar together.

Add one egg and mix until incorporated. Add 2nd egg and mix.

Add Ricotta, salt, Vanilla, and Orange Zest in the mixing bowl with creamed butter and mix until all are completely incorporated.

In another bowl, sift flour, baking soda, and baking powder together.

Add flour and mix just until the flour has completely incorporated into the egg mixture. Do not over-mix.

Heat oven to 325 degrees. Grease 2 cookie pans with butter.

Scoop a heaping tablespoon of dough onto cookie pan to form a cookie. Repeat until all the dough is gone. Bake in a 325 oven until cookies get a slight browned edge, about 14-15 minutes.

Let cookies completely cool. When cool, sprinkle powdered sugar over cookies and serve.

BAZZY'S ITALIAN WEDDING COOKIES

It seems as though there are a number of cultures that make these tasty Almond Cookies. In Russia they're called Russian Tea Cake, both the Mexicans & Italians call them Wedding Cookies, and they're also known as Butterballs, and Snowballs obviously for the heavy dusting of Powdered Sugar that looks just like freshly fallen Snow. My sister Barbara, a.k.a. Bazzy made the best ones I've ever had. Her recipe follows.

RECIPE:

1 & ½ cups Unsalted Butter, softened
¾ cup Powdered Sugar (10X)
¼ teaspoon Salt
1 & ½ cups finely ground Almonds
1 teaspoon Pure Vanilla Extract
3 cups All Purpose Flour
½ cup Powdered Sugar to roll Cookies in

Put butter in a mixing bowl, and gradually add the Powered Sugar.

Beat with electric mixer until it is of a fluffy consistency.

Add Almonds & Vanilla and mix well. Heat oven to 325 degrees. Grease a large cookie sheet pan.

Take a teaspoon of dough and shape into balls (or Crescents), until all the dough is used up. Place on cookie pan and bake till slightly brown, about 14-16 minutes.

Let the cookies cool slightly, but while still warm, roll each cookie in the Powdered Confectionary Sugar.

Let the cookies cool, and roll in sugar again. They're now ready to serve.

ANGINETTI
Neapolitan Lemon Cookies

Aginetti. Lemon Cookies. I just love them. They're a specialty in Naples and the surrounding area of the Amalfi Coast where Lemon Trees abound, and of which the lemons go into the making of the local Lemoncello as well as for millions of serving of Lemon Granita, Lemonade, and various sweets like these tasty Lemon Cookies known as Aginetti. Try them, and dream of the Amalfi Coast as you do. Or Sicily of course, where they're made as well.

COOKIE DOUGH :

½ cup Granulated Sugar
¾ of a stick of Butter
3 large Eggs
1 tablespoon Lemon Extract
2 cups All Purpose Flour
Baking Powder
1/8 teaspoon Salt

FROSTING :

2 ½ cups Confectioners Sugar
1 teaspoon Lemon Extract & ¼ cup Water

Preheat oven to 325 degrees. Grease a cookie sheet with Crisco or pan spray.

In an electric mixer, cream together the ¾ of a stick of Butter, the Sugar, and Lemon Extract until fluffy, about 4 minutes.

With mixer on slow speed add eggs 1 and mix until the egg is completed incorporated. Add the second egg and mix until incorporated and do the same with the 3rd egg.

Mix salt, flour, and Baking powder together in a smaller bowl. Mix the flour slowly into the egg mixture in three equal parts one at a time.
If you have a small scooper (or Tablespoon), scoop some dough onto the cookie pan 1 at a time until all the dough is used up.

Bake cookies in oven at 325 degrees until the cookies just barely start getting lightly brown on the edges, about 12-15 minutes. Remove from the oven and let cook on the side.

For frosting, combine the Confectioners Sugar, water, and Lemon Extract and mix until smooth. Frost the tops of the cookies. Let the frosting dry a few minutes before serving.

ZABAIONE
Sicilian Marsala Wine Custard

8 Egg Yolks
½ cup Granulated Sugar
1 cup Sweet Marsala Wine
1 pint fresh Strawberries, washed and quartered
9 Ladyfingers (optional)

To make this dish you need a double boiler. You can make one by placing a medium pot filled half-way with water, and placing over it a stainless steal mixing bowl that is wider than the pot, so when its place on top of the pot, it won't fall into the pot, but set on top of it.

To make the Zabione, have the water in the pot come to the boil, then lower the heat so the water is at a slight simmer. Place the SS Bowl on top of the pot and add the Egg Yolks, Sugar, and Marsala Wine to the bowl.

Beat with a Wire Whip until the contents becomes a thick creamy fluffy custard, about 7-8 minutes.

Break all the Ladyfingers in half and place 3 pieces in each of 6 Wine Glasses. Equally distribute the Strawberries into the 6 glasses. Fill each glass to the top with Zabaione and serve.

Grandma Bellino's Italian Cookbook

Daniel Bellino Z

ESPRESSO NAPOLETANA
How to Make Espresso in a Napoletana

Espresso? It's *bigger than big in Italy*. Bigger? We're talking about popularity here. There's at least one caffe on almost every block of any city on the Italian Peninsular, a caffe where you can always get a perfectly pulled Espresso. Yes, Italians do love their espresso. It's a big thing in Italian-America as well, though nowhere near to the extent it is in Italy. Never-the-less, *we do love our dark Espresso* brew. And here again in America and among Italian-Americans, it's more of a guy thing than with the ladies. Not that the ladies don't drink it, it's just not in as great of numbers as it is among the male of the species, just as it is with Sausage & Peppers, and the good ole Meatball Parm, it's more of a guy thing, an *Italian guy thing* that is. I, myself, ever since I was a young boy, I had a fascination with my aunts making coffee, whether it was my Aunt Fran making American Coffee in a Percolator Coffee Pot, which I loved watching the coffee percolate in the top glass part of this coffee apparatus that filled the air with the most wonderful sort of coffee aromas imaginable. I tell you, when coffee is made in a percolator pot, it fills your house with the most tantalizing aromas you can ever wish to savor, "I just love it!" And of course, I was majorly fascinated by that weird looking contraption that mu aunts would make *espresso* in. It is contraption only an Italian family would have. It was the famed pot called the *Napoletana*, or as it is known in Italy a

Macchinetta or Cuccumella. Anyway, we're gonna talk about espresso and a thing called a *Napoletana* by Italian-Americans here in America. "No, not a person from Naples, Italy," but a coffee pot. This is a pot made specifically for making Italian Espresso coffee at home. Now, first off it was invented by, not an Italian but a Frenchman named Morize ("Oh my word?"). The full name of this contraption is a Macchinetta Napoletana. Originally the name was probably just a Macchinetta, and people seem to think it became known as a Napoletana rather than a Macchinetta as a result of its great popularity in the southern Italian City of Napoli.

To make an Espresso in a Napoletana, *First*, you take the top pot and fill it with water.

Next, place ground espresso in the filter part of the Napoletana, then place it over the part that has the water in it.

Third, screw the last piece onto the bottom one.

Fourth, place the completed pot on top of a stove and turn the flame on. Let water come to the boil.

Fifth, once the water comes to the boil, take the pot off the heat, then flip the pot over so the boiled water will filter down through the ground espresso, thus making the Espresso coffee. This will take about 5 minutes or so.

Finally, once all the water has dripped down, the Espresso is ready to serve. Serve in demitasse cups, along with sweets if you like, sugar, and or Anisette on the side.

Of course you can have an Espresso on its own, which one often does, but with an array of Italian Cookies and Pastries like, Cannoli, Sfogiatelle, Cookies, and Anisette Toast. Now I ask, "who wouldn't be in 7th Heaven?"

Grandma Bellino's Italian Cookbook

MILLE GRAZIA !!!

Daniel Bellino Z

Grandma Bellino's Italian Cookbook

by The Same Author

SUNDAY SAUCE
When Italian-Americans Cook

SEGRETO ITALIANO
Secret Italian Recipes

THE FEAST of THE 7 FISH
Italian Christmas

La TAVOLA
Italian-American New Yorkers
Adventures of The Table

GOT ANY KAHLUA?

aka

The BIG LEBOWSKI
COOKBOOK

Daniel Bellino Z

BASTA !!!

e

BASTA la PASTA !!!

Printed in Great Britain
by Amazon